Where to Go From Here

BETTY SMITH-SCHUTTE

ISBN: 1456461532
ISBN-13: 9781456461539

Understanding Alcoholism
(A Questionnaire)

	TRUE	FALSE
1. Involuntary treatment of an un-motivated alcoholic has been show to be effective in many cases.	_____	_____
2. Al-Anon is the companion group to Alcoholics Anonymous (AA) for female alcoholics.	_____	_____
3. Alcoholics often seek help for emotional or family problems without ever mentioning a drinking problem to the interviewer.	_____	_____
4. Education about alcoholism often helps alcoholics reduce resistance to accepting the facts about their condition.	_____	_____
5. The alcoholic who is maintaining sobriety has no greater number of serious emotional problems than the population in general.	_____	_____
6. Alcoholism can be seen as a type of drug addiction.	_____	_____

	TRUE	**FALSE**
7. A significant emotional problem or disorder precedes the development of alcoholism.	_____	_____
8. Physicians frequently misdiagnose psychiatric problems in alcoholic persons.	_____	_____
9. Cross-dependency (or cross addiction) to other sedative or tranquilizing drugs in the alcoholic may be induced inadvertently by physicians.	_____	_____
10. The incidence of alcoholism and drug dependence is lower among physicians than the general population.	_____	_____

1. *Involuntary treatment of an unmotivated alcoholic has been shown to be effective in many cases.*

TRUE: Contrary to popular belief, motivation is not essential prior to treatment. There is much evidence that many, if not most, alcoholics become motivated during treatment rather than before. In fact, many "voluntary" patients submit to treatment initially only as a way of coping with strong social pressure of external coercion. Alcoholism almost by definition is an "insight less" illness whose victims are usually unaware of their disorder. To wait until the alcoholic person says "I need to be treated" usually results in such delay as to make death or significant physical and mental deterioration the likely alternative.

2. *Al-Anon is the companion group to Alcoholics Anonymous (AA) for female alcoholics.*

FALSE: Al-Anon is an independent organization parallel in form to AA but for family or friends of the alcoholic. Family members of friends may receive help in Al-Anon through information, support and the guiding philosophy available whether or not the alcoholic is involved in helping him or herself.

3.   *Alcoholics often seek help for emotional or family problems without ever mentioning a drinking problem to the interviewer.*

FALSE: Symptoms such as depression, anxiety, insomnia and psychosomatic ailments as well as marital or family conflicts may be directly related to alcoholic problems which are never spontaneously revealed. It is not uncommon even for the spouse of the alcoholic to ignore or minimize the role of drinking because of the moral stigma of alcoholism and may prefer to see the drinking behavior as a voluntary act of "merely a symptom." In practice, many of all of the problems may be the result of the alcoholism process itself.

4.   *Education about alcoholism often helps alcoholics reduce resistance to accepting the facts about their condition.*

TRUE: Almost invariably, alcoholics in their denial system will believe that an "alcoholic" is someone more severely affected than them. When objectively presented with an education showing the facts about the illness, its nature, symptoms, progression and treat ability, they will often eventually recognize and accept this problem and be motivated to change.

5. ***The alcoholic who is maintaining sobriety has no greater number of serious emotional problems than the population in general.***

TRUE: Sober alcoholics reflect the entire spectrum of psychological adjustment from the "normal" and healthy personality to the psychotically disturbed. Alcoholism has been found to exist in persons suffering from all known mental illnesses as well as in persons who have no other detectable mental or psychiatric disorder. The latter situation is the usual on in that, apart from mild personality problems, the typical alcoholic person does not have significant psychiatric illness.

6. ***Alcoholism can be seen as a type of drug addiction.***

TRUE: The World Health Organization defines drug addition as a state of chronic or periodic intoxication detrimental to the individual or society, characterized by:
> 1) An overpowering desire to take the drug no matter how it must be obtained,
> 2) A tendency to increase the dose, and

3) Psychological and sometimes physical dependency upon the effects of the drug. Certainly, alcoholism fits this definition.

7.   *A significant emotional problem or disorder generally precedes the development of alcoholism.*

FALSE: The use of alcohol by an alcoholic person can be productive of anxiety and depression and may also bring out psychological mechanisms and traits that are not apparent without alcohol. For this reason, assessment of the psychiatric status of the alcoholic when done during active drinking or in the early withdrawal stages can be grossly misleading. Psychiatric assessment should properly be done both during active drinking and in the state of sobriety.

8.   *Physicians frequently misdiagnose psychiatric problems in alcoholic persons.*

TRUE: The use of alcohol by an alcoholic person can be productive of anxiety and depression and may also bring out psychological mechanisms and traits that are not apparent without alcohol. For this reason, assessment of the psychiatric status of the alcoholic when done during active drinking or in the early withdrawal stages can be grossly misleading. Psychiatric assessment should properly be done both during active drinking and in the state of sobriety.

9.   *Cross-dependency (or cross addition) to other sedative or tranquilizing drugs in the alcoholic may be induced inadvertently by a physician.*

TRUE: Probably the most common criticism of the way physicians manage alcoholic person is the tendency to prescribe medications which, in fact, may result in additional drug dependency problems. At times, alcoholic persons attempt to manipulate their physicians into prescribing these drugs for their known euphoric and mood-altering effects. Such cross-dependency is so common that it must be investigated in any person suspected of alcoholism.

10.   *The incidence of alcoholism and drug dependence is lower among physicians than the general population.*

FALSE: Estimates of physician addiction rates are higher than those of the general population. In a Mayo Clinic study, Duffy found alcoholism or drug dependence to be in the major disorder in 50 per cent of all physicians admitted to the psychiatric unit. State boards of medical examiners in Arizona and Oregon report 2 per cent of practicing physicians were subject to disciplinary action for drug dependence over a period of ten years.

As a teenager, I began a slow process of self-destruction. The method I chose was effective but not unique. Thousands of teenagers just like me have taken the same path. Psychologists are not sure why it happens, but for her it was a desperate cry for recognition and understanding. As a routine social drink that quickly snowballs into an all-consuming, self-destruction obsession.

Some other symptoms of the disease include physiological changes, such as: loss of weight, or just the opposite, gaining weight, cessation of the menstrual cycle, hair loss, waste of muscle tissue, low basal metabolic rate, anemia, sleep disturbances, low or high blood pressure, slow pulse, low body temperature and kidney dysfunction. The doctors seem to read a simple "malnutrition" rather than the "alcohol malnutrition."

The problem today is that social drinking is more accepted among women, inebriation is not. Alcoholism is an illness, but treated as a disgrace by the unknowing public. An alcoholic is emotionally, spiritually, morally, sometimes physically and possibly financially bankrupt. Even though it is bad for a man it is considered twice as bad for a woman. Drunken behavior in a man is accepted but not in a woman. This in turn leaves the woman lonely, isolated and feeling of guilt and will not seek help for her problem. She in turn becomes secretive about her drinking problem. Usually, her problem is overlooked by relatives and friends as well as denied and also this is done so as to protect her from the social stigmatization. Since the use of alcoholic beverages in any society is part of the culture, the female alcoholic remains on the fringe of the mainstream society and non-alcoholic.

After going to detox it is highly recommended for women to go to a halfway house environment (rehabilitation) for 90 days just to learn how to cope with the sober life as well as her family and friends. The family usually refuses to be counseled as to how to help her cope with life. Suicide is very high in the female alcoholic after she gets detox. The halfway house setting helps her overcome the stigmatization and it teaches her coping strategies that enable her to adapt to their discrediting status.

This is a story which is very hard for me to tell as there are some things I did that society today wouldn't accept and of course that is good. The most important thing for a girl growing up is to gain respect for her soul as well as her body. It would be nice to be grown up and mature all at once but that would be boring. God keeps putting babies on this earth and that's God's opinion that the world should go on. My reason for telling this story is to help other women no matter what age to understand their changes and to accept life just as it comes naturally and not try to be someone they are not. My lesson learned from experience is that when it doesn't feel right, be yourself and don't do it. It's OK to say No. Boy! If I only knew that when I was growing up.

CHAPTER 1

My Childhood Background

Here's a little background about me. I was born in a small town in the Shenandoah Valley called Harrisonburg, Virginia. I was a fat tow-headed blue eyed baby. It will be hard to tell about my first years, but I will tell it as I was told. We lived in a very small neighborhood, clean and respectful. I was the third child of all girls. The first sister died at birth. The second sister is four years older than me.

Starting from when I entered Kindergarten, in a small town, I was always afraid to be away from my mother, and my mother had a tough time convincing me that it was OK to go to school, and be away from her to learn and get smart. I can remember when I was determined to go home and be with my mother one day, the teacher had put us all in the classroom down to nap, on our individual mats, and she left the room. Well, of course I wanted to be with my mother, so I got up and walked out of the school and went home. The only thing was that when I got there, my mother wasn't home. I heard the washing machine going, but didn't know where she was. Of course, knowing that I had done wrong by walking home without permission and naturally being afraid of being alone....I just sat down and cried. My mother was next door and when she came home and found me sitting there, she immediately called the school and told them I was home, then she proceeded to scold me. As time went on, as you will see that I always was determined to do what I wanted, regardless of it being right or wrong. I just did it because it was what I wanted, and it wasn't always right. I was very hard-headed.

When we, my sister and I, were ages 6 and 10, my mother started us in taking piano and violin lessons, just up the street from where we lived. Even though we were poor, my mother managed to take in washing and ironing to make extra money to pay bills and give us what was needed to keep up with the Jones. She also cleaned houses for people. Daddy never kept a steady job because of his drinking.

Back to the music lessons, our teacher would put us in this cold room to practice and to this day I don't know why except that I guess she expected that if we wanted to keep warm we had to practice fast and get warm that way. My sister and I both hated this. After a lot of practice we evidently became very good as we played on the local radio program which included playing for special occasions. One in particular was a wedding, I was requested to play the piano and of course I was so nervous that I got stuck playing the bridal march, I kept playing over and over again the same thing until the music teacher came to assist me and then I went on with the show OK.

Coming from an average middle class family we lived well with the help of my mother's extra side jobs as my father drank all the time and was very mean to my mother and us kids when he got drunk. My mother played the mother/father image to us kids. Rather than calling us kids all through this story I intend to give us names, which are not our real names, to protect us from some embarrassment as this is a true story of what actually happened in my life. We will call me Teri and my sister Gloria.

When payday came my dad would always get drunk and spend the money or lose it somehow. So my mother had to go where dad worked and get the money, before he spent it, to buy groceries and pay bills. Most of the time they would argue as he always owed someone money for his booze he borrowed during the week. When we left dad, we would go grocery shopping and window shop a little. From time to time mother would buy material to make our clothes to keep up with the latest style. We never went without anything or hungry. Actually, the upbringing was no different then the average family except that my father had a drinking problem which

made it hard to live a normal life. The environment was always upsetting; my mother and father were always screaming at each other and
fighting. My father would also scream at Gloria
and me as well.

There seemed to be a definite psychological as
well as a physical problem in my early years. The
fear I had as a young girl was that all men were
like my father. Funny, that when you grow up in
a certain environment, you actually mold your
life to that as a way of life, unless you are lucky
to get help and get away. I was a very insecure
person. Only my mother would convince me to
the fact that everything was OK.

When I was six years old we moved to Alexandria, Virginia. My father moved there first and
got a job and a place to live and then sent
for us. When we got there it was plain to see
that he arranged to have everything comfortable for himself, certainly not us. He found a
place up over a store on the main street which
overlooked a bar across the street. Gloria and
I played out back in the alley. The place was
infested with roaches. When my mother saw this
she immediately began to clean the place up
and before long there were no more bugs and
the apartment was spic and span. Mother was
always a fanatic about cleanliness.

We met one of dad's friend's family, who was a fellow worker. Nina and Paul and their two girls. Nina and Paul were outgoing people and lots of fun. Paul drank with dad a lot and Nina worked as a waitress with not much time to be a mother and a housewife. She asked my mother to take care of her children and clean her house and of course mother accepted and got paid well for it. Mother liked Nina very much as she always got mother laughing and took mother and us places along with her two girls when she wasn't working.

Soon again dad's drinking caused him to lose his job as he would show up drunk on the job and the man told my mother that he couldn't have him drunk around the job. Dad's luck again ran out. He was such a good mechanic that he was never out of a job for very long. He got another job down the road out of the city limits. It was a job running a gas station and doing mechanical work on cars for a salary plus an apartment in the back of the station. We moved again and started all over once more. Mother, Gloria and I adjusted somehow. The gas station had a small store in it also a small restaurant. The lady that owned it was always kidding Gloria and I about eating our breakfast. She would say that if we ate all of our food that she would give us ice cream. Believe me we ate the whole breakfast just to get the ice cream. She was always giving us goodies from the store, providing that we were good girls. Mother sure was happy as we were always good.

While we lived there dad continued to drink but this lady (the owner) kept him in line. She would watch him closely and give him some to drink and wouldn't let him have much to drink during the day. This worked for a while. We lived this lifestyle for a while.

Suddenly, one day we got a call from my grand-mother that my grandfather (on my mother's side of the family) was dying and to come home immediately. Well, Mother, Gloria and I went. Grandfather died the next day. We stayed there for a few days and the third day we got a call from dad saying that he lost his job and to stay where we were until he got another job. We decided to stay with our Aunt Dorothy who was real nice to us. Mother enrolled us in this little three room schoolhouse. It was so peace-ful living in the country. It was also fun going to that little 3 room school. I wasn't afraid of people living there. A few months went by and dad sent for us. Again, we moved back to the big city. This time we found a nice new town-house right at the end of the road near the railroad tracks. It had a nice yard with a small creek along side the house where my sister and I would go and catch tadpoles and keep them in a fish bowl until they grew legs and turned into frogs and then we would put them back into the creek.   This was a very nice place to live. My Mother was happy but as usual Dad got drunk again using up all the money, so mother returned to the washing, ironing and cleaning houses to survive. This time she had to rent out rooms in the house to make enough money to pay the bills. Dad was working for the airlines at the airport painting the decals and signs on the airplanes. He said that he couldn't stand the smell of the paint anymore and had to quit. Again, he wasn't out of work for long until he found a good job not too far from the house working for a car dealership. He made pretty good money. Mother still had to go and meet him on paydays as that were the only way she got some money to get groceries and pay bills.

I somehow just couldn't adjust to the constant moving as I developed stomach problems and mother had to take me to the doctors. The doctor told mother that I had a nervous stomach and gave me medicine to take to tranquilize my stomach so I could digest my food properly. Being sick all the time I was afraid to go to school for fear of getting sick and so my mother to walk me to school everyday and stay for a while with me until I felt secure there.

I met a real nice girl that lived across the street and her family would invite me over a lot to eat.

I really liked to go over there, as a matter of fact; I would stay until it was time for me to go to bed. I really didn't want to go home for fear of mother and dad still arguing. I wanted so bad to stay there where it was so peaceful, without arguing and fighting.

One of the roomer's was my Dad's sister that had a drinking problem also. It helped with the rent and she finally got just like Dad, she lost her job and stayed drunk all the time. We were always upset by her and dad arguing with mother. Mother finally ended up kicking her out. We got another roomer and he also had a drinking problem. He would come home from work and drink so much that he would hallucinate. He would call us into his room and tell us to get the pink elephants off the walls so he could go to sleep, of course, there weren't any elephants on the wall. Mother finally kicked him out.

By this time we were into World War II and the Depression. We were rationed with stamps for meat, sugar, flour, etc. Once a month we could get a 5 pound bag of sugar and the same with the meat and flour. I remember when we went to the grocery store and mother ran back to get her sugar before it was all gone and left me in charge to watch it. Well, I got distracted and someone stole it so we had to use brown sugar the whole month. It was hard times now. We had meat twice a month and beans and much (liquid cornmeal) dipped in milk for the rest of the month. Finally, the war was over. I remember some people coming to the house and talking to mother and dad about buying the house as the owner died. Dad said that we couldn't afford to buy it so we had to move as the servicemen were coming home from the war and the owner intended to sell the house to the GI's. We moved to another house, actually it was a second floor apartment with a side porch downstairs. It was nice. My sister and I really liked this place as we had plenty of nice friends. Dad continued to change jobs but doing better with the money. Mother and Dad were looking for a house closer to the high school. They found a duplex house in a nice residential neighborhood and rented it. It had three bedrooms upstairs, a real large house with a front porch. My sister and I shared a room and mother rented out the third bedroom. We really like this house.

By this time my sister was working after school everyday and on weekends to have spending money. I liked what I saw and wanted the same. I lied about my age when I was 14 and had changed my birth certificate to say that I was 16. The school board where you had to get a working permit evidently didn't check with the school because they automatically gave me a work permit. I was so happy. I applied for a part-time job where my sister worked and got it. This also helped out at home as mother didn't have to buy us our extras anymore and we bought some of our own clothes. By now I was beginning to like the freedom that I had at such a young age. I was very confused and disturbed at this time also. The going to school with kids my age wasn't fun anymore as I had a taste of the older crowd and liked it. I grew up too fast but still wasn't matured to handle it. I started dressing older and wearing lots of makeup. Everyone thought I was older, especially the guys. I started going out with different guys that I met at the servicemen's lounge where I became a hostess with the consent of my parents. So all I was doing was going to school, then work, and then to the lounge and dancing everyday. I loved dancing. This was my recreation, and I got pretty good at dancing. This servicemen's lounge became an obsession with me. I liked how the men were treating me, like I was somebody. The only bad part at this point of my life was that I knew nothing about sex. I can remember when my mother bought two different kinds of napkins and she would put one kind down stairs in the kitchen and another upstairs in the linen closet. When I asked why she said the ones upstairs were for when we ran out of toilet paper. I believed that for a long time. Mother never was comfortable around me when I asked her about sex. She would change the subject or say you are too young to be thinking about sex. So the way I found out about sex was from kids at school who had already tried it. Unfortunately, I learned from the fast girls and older men. From then on I figured I knew it all. On Friday and Saturday nights I would go out after the servicemen's lounge closed. I met a lot of people there, men as well as girl friends. I let one of the guys walk me home one night and because I wouldn't give him sex he told me that he wouldn't go out with me again until I decided to have sex with him. The next day at school and at work both I asked the girls is that a fact and they said of course. They said in order to keep a guy I had to give him sex. At first I didn't believe that as some girls told me not to believe that. I accepted a date with a few more guys and the same thing happened. By this time I was convinced that it was true.

The funny thing was I had heard men and women at the lounge talking about This certain girl and how no good she was for going out with any man that would have her. To me she looked popular. So I finally let one of the guys try to have sex. My first time was very scary and painful. I was frantic and all this guy did was laugh at me. I finally got up nerve enough to ask some girls at school as I was scared. They said that I was no longer a virgin and the next time it wouldn't hurt it would feel good. I still didn't know too much so I looked up the word virgin in the dictionary to see

what it meant. Then I became very depressed.
The next few weeks I kind of stayed away from
the lounge and when I did go back everyone
was glad to see me. The girls said they heard
what had happened to me. I was so upset that I
ran all the way home.

CHAPTER 2

Introduction to my First Part-Time Job

I continued to go through the motions of functioning my daily chores and responsibilities until one day I decided that I was grown up enough to handle life. I was working part-time at a clothing store where the owner of the store kept telling me that I should be a model. He kept getting me to try on certain clothes and when they didn't fit up top he informed me to add a little more padding where it was needed. At Christmas time he asked me and the other sales ladies to model clothes for his special men only night party for them to view the apparel for ideas to buy their wives and girlfriends presents. He sold a lot of clothing. He also let us keep what we modeled. I modeled a black and white satin lounge pants and jacket. While I worked there I bought a lot of clothes during the summer as I worked full time and saved up enough money to go to Patricia Stevens Modeling School in Washington, DC. I enjoyed that very much. I couldn't afford to go through the whole course, but wanted very much to be a model. I took the $300 course which was personal improving. The whole time I went my sister laughed at me. I asked mother to help me pay for the modeling school and she said that she just couldn't afford it. My sister thought that I was crazy wanting to be a model as she thought I was too skinny and ugly. She always laughed at me.

By this time my sister convinced my mother to rent out the room to her fiancé. She and he both worked for the government in the Pentagon. Well, he was living in our house also and keeping Dad occupied, with his drinking, I was getting guidance from him as well of which I did not want. You see my sister's boyfriend kept telling me that I was all grown up. Finally, sister and her fiancé got married and moved out. Now I had the bedroom to myself. I continued to do things my way and was hardly ever home. Mother complained but really didn't do much about it. I know that she worried a lot I was afraid to bring anybody home for fear that my Dad would be drinking and embarrass me. Finally I graduated and got myself a job at the government in the Pentagon. I still kept my part-time job along with my full-time job as a secretary for the government in the Pentagon.

I met a nice girlfriend at work and as we talked about our problems at home we agreed to go out and rent an apartment together. She had two kids, a boy and a girl. We agreed to let the kids have one bedroom and we shared the other one. She furnished all of the furniture except the bedroom set. Well, starting right off this wasn't working as her boyfriend drank heavy and would come over and beat her up just like I had at home. So eventually, I asked a lawyer if I could break my lease and he said to get the furniture store where I bought the bedroom suit to go by when my roommate was home and pick up my furniture and to tell her that I reneged paying on my bill and they were repossessing it. It worked and I had it delivered back to my parent's house. I moved back into my room and gave that new bedroom suite to mother and dad, a present for letting me come back home. I also bought them a new TV as theirs went on the blink.

This girl, my ex-roommate had the nerve to come to my work and tell me that I had to pay the rent but I informed her that she had better talk to my lawyer which scared her off and eventually her boyfriend moved in the apartment to help her. I told her that her boyfriend was the reason why I moved out and that the main reason for me getting the apartment with her was to get away from the drinking environment and that if I was going to put up with that kind of a problem it would be my father rather than her boyfriend. She finally left me alone. I sure learned my lesson, never to move in with a roommate.

I went and borrowed enough money to buy myself a nice used car, a 1950 Buick. Now I was really independent. I started going over to DC after work dancing and drinking. Having a real ball. Meeting lots of people. I met a nice guy that was in a click of good dancers. I was so happy that I got accepted in the click. Now I felt that I was really somebody. Little did I know that this was the beginning of my trouble. It all happened so innocently. We dated or met there quite a bit, at the dance hall until he asked where I lived and I told him in VA. He came over and met me and took me out first in VA. It turned out that he was from VA also and knew quite a few people in the bars that I frequented quite a bit. Well, when we walked in all eyes were on us. We danced every dance. This was a private club as VA had no dancing allowed in the state unless it was a private club. The VA guys came over to say hello. They seemed to know this guy quite well. Up to now no one really knew me or cared whether I existed or not. This guy that I was with was well known, what a shock, all of a sudden I became well known as well. I didn't care how he became so popular I was just glad to finally become one of the popular bunch. We traveled back and forth from DC to VA going to every dance hall there was. We both seemed to be popular on the dance floor as our style was the "in style" (DC style they called it). People would move off the dance floor to watch us dance. One night this couple, a man and his wife, approached us about teaching them to dance this style. We went to their house in Maryland to try and breakdown the style to teach. They were both instructors at Fred Astairs Dance Studio. After numerous attempts we found it impossible to breakdown to teach. So that ended real quick.

I was beginning to like this guy very much. When he found that I was falling for him he informed me that he was married but he was trying to get a divorce from his wife who was running around on him with his best friend. We saw her and her boyfriend out where we would go dancing and he would take me along with him to check up on his wife. Because he was so truthful about this I continued to date him. I really fell in love with him. He was into drugs as well as alcohol pretty heavy. He introduced me to pot. I really didn't like it, it made me feel very paranoid. This fantasy soon came to an end when I got a phone call one night from his wife asking me if I had seen him. I told her no that I had no idea where he was. Then she proceeded to tell me that they found his car at the marina close to the airport and had no idea where he was. Later, I found out that he temporarily had a lose of memory, parked his car at the marina and walked to the airport nearby and caught a flight to Florida. After this ordeal he went back with his wife. I was very hurt, lonely, and depressed.

CHAPTER 3

The Beginning

In order to keep myself occupied I started a part-time job to accommodate my lifestyle. I traded my car for a little later model. After work I would go dancing in VA and DC. I would get home just in time to change clothes and go to my full-time job. This went on and progressively things got confusing. I met a lot of people that were involved with drugs. This one girl would ask me to take her to the doctors supposedly to get a shot (allergy shot she said) but I later found out that she was doing things in the doctors office with him while I waited in the waiting room and in turn he would give her pills of which I also found out that she sold on the street. I told her that I didn't want to lose my job with the government and that I would no longer take her there. I met another guy in DC and thought he was a nice guy but he turned out to be involved with drugs as well. I stopped going to those places in DC. I came back to VA clubs and of course they weren't as advanced as I had been used too. They asked me where I learned to dance and I said DC. These guys I met wanted to learn to dance like me. So I took them to DC. This was fun. One of them I got to like very much. We went to DC a lot but he would always meet me at certain places in VA. I finally realized why because he had other girlfriends and didn't want them to know that he was going to DC with me. I accepted this like a dummy. I was having too much fun to be tied down.

Well, we became very well acquainted with each other and one thing led to another. Before you knew it I was pregnant. I went to him and told him that I was pregnant and he said that it wasn't his baby. I told him that it was and I needed help. Well, very quickly he disappeared out of sight. I was working for the government then and I knew that if I was pregnant working for the government and not married that would lose my job. So without checking into it I quit the government when I was 3 months pregnant. What led to this was that I finally began to show some symptoms of pregnancy and my mother approached me, at first I denied it until I knew I had to admit it. I tried for two months to get rid of the baby but couldn't. I cried when I told my mother and as you well know she was very upset, but handled it well with me. I felt so bad as this was humiliating for her and my whole family. She told my dad who stayed drunk most of the time anyway. When he got drunk he would call me a whore. After a few weeks passed he told me that we would make the best of it.

We moved to another house downtown. I went to the Alexandria clinic to have my baby and the counselor there told me that I would have to give up my car and fur coat, neither of which was paid for yet. In talking with her she said that if I had any belongings that were worth anything and also that if I lived at home that it was my family's responsibility to help. That I didn't qualify for state help. She also asked me who the father was and I refused to tell her, at this point she told me that they couldn't help. I cried all the way home. Mother was upset now because she couldn't afford to pay the bill. My sister and brother-in-law who lived in Arlington suggested that I come and live with them and go to the Arlington Clinic and tell them that I lived in Arlington. I went to the Arlington Clinic and they said no problem that they would accept me and when I went back to work that I could pay them back if I wanted to but it was not necessary. Well, I realistically stayed with mother and dad.

As time went on every time I would go to the clinic my mother said that this man and woman would come by the house to see her. They tried to talk her into convincing me to give up my baby. They said that they would pay for my hospital bill as well as give me some money for the baby. I told my counselor at the hospital and they called the police about this as there was a couple going around in the area approaching young unwed pregnant girls like me, trying to buy their babies. I went home and told my mother and dad about this and they laughed. About a week later I came home from a part-time job and there was two detectives sitting there talking to my mother and dad. First of all in front of the two detectives my dad apologized for not believing me and the two detectives proceeded to talk to me about what kind of people these two were. He explained that they would humiliate the girl and impress her that she could make money and also have a place to go until she had the baby, then sell the baby to them. The detectives asked me to call them every time I went anywhere. I agreed. I also told them that when I was returning from a babysitting job one night that a car tried to run me off of the road. The detectives said that that had happened to another girl and she wrecked her car and was hurt very bad. So I agreed to call them every time I went anywhere.

The ninth month had finally arrived and while I was in the hospital having the baby the detectives came to visit and told me that they caught those people. I sure was glad. There was a big write up in the social paper about them. When I left the hospital I moved back in with mother and dad. I really was happy that I was able to keep my baby, but soon the newness wore off and I wanted to go out and party. First I went back to work at the Pentagon for the government. Dad kept telling me that he wanted to love my baby

but when babies are small that he was afraid
of them and when my little girl grew up that he
would hold her and acknowledge her more.

The old routine soon resumed. Every weekend I
still had to drive mother to where dad worked to
get his money before he would spend it all. Dad
would come home drinking every night. Mother
had him locked up a few times when he got violent, hoping to force him to quit drinking. One Friday evening dad came home from work almost
sober for a change. It was a hot day and dad
always liked to go down into the recreation room
to sleep as it was cooler down there. Mother
and I were sitting in the living room watching TV
when he came in. He went upstairs and used
the bathroom and when he came down he
stumbled and lost his balance, but he still didn't
seem drunk. He walked through the living room
and through the dining room OK and went
through the kitchen. I asked dad if he needed
help to get down those basement stairs as he has
stumbled down them before when he was drinking and he said no that he was a big boy and
was capable of handling getting down the stairs
all by himself. No sooner said then done he fell.
Mother and I ran to the top of the stairs and there
he was lying at the foot of the stairs all twisted up.
We ran down to help him and his eyes were open
but he couldn't talk. We lifted him up on the bed
in the basement.

Mother talked to him and he moaned just like he would do when he was drinking. She said that he was drunk and not to worry, for me to go on out as I had planned. Well, I did but I told her to call me if he seemed worse. Mother called me at the club where I was and ask me to come home quick. When I got there she said the she had been talking to him but he would only moan. She said she laid down beside him and held his hand. She asked him if he had to go to the bath-room and told him to go in the bed. She said that he did and this alerted her that something was wrong as dad never did wet the bed. We called the rescue ambulance and they took him to the hospital. When we got there they asked if we had a family doctor. We said no as dad never did get sick to go to a doctor. They called in the house doctor (an intern). He told us after asking a few questions that dad was only drunk. We insisted that he wasn't as he had fallen down a flight of stairs. They released him and told us to keep an eye on him and bring him back if he didn't seem any better. My friends that were with me said no way that they weren't a doc-tor but they knew that there was something wrong. Well, this was about 2:00 AM and we took him home. We had to carry him out as he was still unconscious. At 6:00 AM mother woke me up crying and said that dad was bleed-ing through the roots of his hair in one spot and blood was running out of his nose. We called

the ambulance again and it was the same driver
and they said that they were not supposed to
give advice but they suggested that we sue the
hospital for negligence. The hospital called in the
best Neuro-Surgeon to look at dad.

In the meantime until he got there for the hospital to X-ray him for preparation for surgery. The
doctor was doing surgery at another hospital
and said that he would be there as soon as he
finished. When the doctor arrived it was noon.
The doctor introduced himself to mother and
me and said that the X-rays weren't clear and
he had to rush and get more done. All that he
could tell us from looking at dad was that he only
had a 50-50 chance, because when he tapped
his spine it contained almost all blood, which
was a bad sign. Dad was in surgery for seven
hours and when he came out he was to have
a full-time nurse watching him as his lungs had
to be pumped out every hour or sooner until he
regained conscious. They could not find a full-
time nurse so mother and I watched and called
the nurse if we heard him wheezing. While we
were sitting there with mother on the one side and
me on the other side of the bed, dad seemed to
be going through the motion of trying to cough
and he moved his head down towards his chest.
I told mother lets go get the doctor or nurse. We
waited outside of his room and when they came
out they said that he was dead. Well, mother and

I went crazy. They had to give mother a sedative and me also. I was raging mad. I went immediately to the phone and called my lawyer and told him about this. He said that I had a pretty good case but he couldn't take it as the hospital did him a few favors and he didn't want to ruin his reputation with them. By this time I was fit to be tied. My sister and brother-in-law were there helping to get mother calmed down to go home. When we got home the hospital called and said that they pronounced dad dead at 7:00 PM. I was in shock and needed a drink bad. When I got home my sister, brother-in-law and I got a good stiff drink. We got mother to lay down and with the sedative that they gave her at the hospital, she fell asleep. I couldn't get over the negligence on the hospital's part. I went back to the hospital alone and asked for the doctor that sent my dad home from the hospital that morning and funny no one knew what doctor it was or where he was. I told them that I intended to sue for negligence. We prepared for the funeral.

After the funeral I tried for weeks to find a lawyer to take my case and not one would do so. Finally, time pasted and it was forgotten. By the way, dad died on Father's Day. I had to take all of his gifts back and this was very depressing. Here I was with a small baby and mother to take care of. I really didn't know what to do or where to start. I felt so insecure.

CHAPTER 4

Spiraling Down

Up to now I think I must have known that mother loved me, but we never spoke of love. All affection in my family was expressed by physical touch – a gentle pat or a hearty hug. Mother did the best she could to nurture me and Sue, my daughter, but she never managed to instill in me the assurance that I was acceptable to anyone outside my home. I never felt I belonged anywhere. With a mother who seemed troubled all the time and with no father figure at all, I felt set apart by my family structure long before I became aware of other shortcomings. I also felt estranged from life by poverty. Poverty was always a significant part of my existence.

Unconsiciously, I began to accept society's evaluation of me as valid. I would have denied it vigorously, but deep within I was beginning to think of myself as inferior. I expected very little from myself and almost nothing from life. I had two dreams struggling to exist in the poor soil of my early years. They were the only goals I can remember having as I grew up.

The first one was to get married and wear a white wedding dress and showing my peers the visible evidence of purity and self-respect. The other goal grew out of my success as a student. I wanted to be a teacher when I grew up. I suppose this was still wanting to be accepted and respected.

Later, I found out that all the bills that were in dad's name had to be paid and mother couldn't pay them so I had to start paying all of them along with the bills that I had incurred. This was a big blow. First, of all I had just gotten back to work at the Pentagon and had lots of catching up on my own bills. I called my sister and asked her for help and she said in so many words that she had her home and life to take care of and they couldn't help. Well, I got furious. Perhaps I only was reacting to change the way any adolescent, particularly such as an insecure one, might have reacted. The dread I was feeling was just fear of the unknown. I had sensed already that this added responsibility was not going to be a step up in the world for me.

I started going out every night after work hoping to forget my troubles and fears but it only made it worse mentally and physically. Mean while mother and I were not seeing eye to eye on anything. She was forever bugging me about my clothing of behavior. She kept saying, you are going to be somebody someday, I am so proud of you! I could not stand her blind stupidity. What would it take to accept reality? I began to feel contempt, mother was living in a dream world. I was growing tired of pretending to be something I wasn't. I gradually stopped asking permission to go out, instead, I just stayed away from home more and more. The old habits of respect and obedience for my mother as head of my family were broken. The friends I met outside of my home became my family. The guilt set in about mother being left alone with Sue. I didn't stop to think that mother missed dad. People kept telling me that Sue was good therapy for mother to have some one home with her after dad died. I came to recognize that I was the head-of-the-household, being that I had to take responsibilities of all the bills. I felt justified that I had the right to go out if I wanted to. Because you see I never had a close family when dad was living.

We existed but with dad's alcoholism there was no family. Just mother my sister and I. Surviving. I suggested to my mother that we should look for a less expensive place like an apartment with two bedrooms, we certainly didn't need this two story house with the small front and backyard and all the nice things that made mother happy, I knew that I should think of mother's happiness but I figured that I had to make the decision for mother about moving. I now wished I hadn't as mother a loved a yard. All I thought about was something less expensive that I could afford. So we found an apartment back in the Delray section of town. Mother liked it there. She got permission at the resident managers to plant flowers outside apartment window, we had a basement apartment and all she had to do was look out her kitchen window at her beautiful garden. She could reach out and touch them if she wanted to. I think the apartment also made mother get on with her life and forget dad. All she had was good things to say about him even though he mistreated her. I guess she really loved him to put up with all the heartaches. I remember back when she took the advice of a friend to lock dad up when he mistreated her and id one time. We went to court over it and the judge warned him that if he did it again that she was going to lock him up. Well, he did it again and mother had him locked up. The courts ordered him to see a psychiatrist while he was in jail. He did over a period of two weeks. The analysis said that when he was sober he was afraid to talk to the doctor and tell how he felt. The doctor recommended to mother to leave him for her own good. As he never intended to quit drinking. Of course mother loved him and thought that his being in jail would make him change. We went to visit him twice a week and he told mother and I that he liked it there, in jail. He said that he felt good and protected. When he got out he drank again, it never stopped. Mother made up her mind then that she would just put up with it and never lock him up again.

She knew that he was sick and said that the Lord was ready for him. It was for a reason, she always said. I would take mother shopping on Saturdays just like before, also Sue liked to go to the fast food place and eat. On Sundays I would take them for a ride of their choice, just like dad would do. Soon with my enormous thirst and my love of night life, I was back into my usual habits. No one seemed concerned that I was still a minor. I would go to the bar every night joked and laughed with the others there, mostly men, and matched the best of them in drinking beer. By midnight I was smashed. Life didn't seem so bad when it could be kept at a distance with alcohol. Soon I as feeling fretless and angry again. Now I know why the gang I hung around with had gotten into drugs~ it was to combat the nothingness of this existence. Life still centered around bars with crowds of people.

There was no real pleasure in living~ there were no goals ahead. What we seemed to look forward to was just more of the same grinding poverty – for a lifetime.

I was starting to hear a lot of flack from my sister as well as my mother. So we all had a big meeting about what we were to do about me and my attitude. I told my sister that I had too much responsibilitiy and needed help. To start with, help me get out of debt. I convinced them to take some of mothers's money she got out of my car accident to pay them off.

They decided to do so, but I resented the fact that at first my sister didn't want anything to do with helping mother and I out and making it so that I couldn't touch mothers money. They had it so that my brother-in-law was the partner to mother and her money. I was still being treated by my sister as an adolescent and given all of the responsibilities of a full fledged adult. Whatever that was.

You know alcoholics don't make good mothers. The children seem to have for their parents affection. This rival is evil and more powerful than the strongest mothers love. An alcoholic needs for a fix always seems greater and more compelling to her than any need her child might have. Sue was a lucky to have a mother. Mother should not have had to take on yet another child to raise, especially In the view of the heartbreak she had suffered from her attempts to raise me. But she knew, and so did I, that I would be imcompetent as a mother. She accepted the full responsibility for Sue's care. Soon I was nothing more that an occasional visitor to Sue. Now my drinking habit begain to catch up with me.

All my friends said that my situation wa unique but that my mother and sister should have some understanding about my being so young with a child was burdening me. I was so confused about what was right and I began to talk to doctors and they said that I was going through growing up and that to hang in there it would get better. I was on tranquilizers to calm down. This caused by to fall asleep at my work (along with the combination of booze) and the doctor gave me another pill to counteract the tranquilizer. So here I am popping pills and freaking out. A human time bomb. I had gotten to the point that I didn't want any food, I guess it was the combination of the drugs, uppers, downers, anyway I went back to the doctors and told him that I could not swallow solid foods. He gave me another pill to calm down my stomach nerves. This sure shows how little doctors knew about alcoholism or drug addition, and I feel that today they still don't know when to detect an alcoholic.

CHAPTER 5

Risky Behavior

By now I was so hostile toward my sister and mother. The drugs had full control of me. I mistreated my mother, sometimes even hitting her. When I came down from the drugs I realized what I had done and apologized. My drugs changed my personality to the point that I cared nothing about reality and told my mother that I was going to leave if she didn't get off of my back. By this time my sister and brother-in-law came over and had another talk with me in front of my mother about my attitude and responsibilities. I told them that they didn't want to help me when dad died and to keep their nose out of my business. They in so many words told me that if I didn't quit mistreating mother and Sue that they would do something about it. I cried and begged them to help me get out of debt as I couldn't keep going the way I was going and that I would change my ways. I told them that the reason that I was going out every night was to find a man that would marry me and take care of me.

They laughed at me and said that I was going about life all wrong, that my job was to take care of Sue now and looking for a man later. Mother added that I wouldn't find a good man in the bars. She said I would find a good man in church. Of course, I didn't want to go to church because that would mean that I would have to stop drinking and going out and having fun and that wasn't for me at this point. Well, one more time my sister and brother-in-law agreed to get me out of debt. When this got straightened out I still didn't care about anyone but me. I felt confused, I guess my conscious was working on me. I knew this real nice couple that I had met at the bar and they sort of took me under their wings, so to speak. They helped me to face a small portion of reality. I had a flashback to when I was a kid and it seemed that mother never saw any wrong in my sister. My mother always believed that all of the arguments were my fault. I resented the fact that I always got the hand-me-downs because I was smaller and younger. I can remember when my dad bought a dog for us. My sister would get to hold the dog most of the time. So one day I got him and jumped on my tricycle and started peddling, my sister came up from behind me and pushed me down. I was holding on to the dog and when I fell, I fell on my nose. It started bleeding badly, mother asked what happened and I told her, then my sister came in and told her version that I took the dog from her and that's why she pushed me down. Mother just told her never to do that again. I resented this very much. I felt mother loved her more than me and I rebelled from then on every time mother sided with my sister.

Getting back to my problems. I had changed jobs and was working at the Army dispensary as an appointment clerk. Even though I was not a dependent while working there the head of the dispensary said that all civil service employees could pick one doctor in the dispensary and use the facilities free as a dependent. Well, one day I went to talk to this real nice civilian doctor there about my problems. He suggested after listening to my situation that I should consider letting my sister and brother-in-law adopt my daughter Sue. I talked it over with my friends and they said it sounded pretty good. The time had come for me to make a decision and I went along with letting my sister adopt Sue. Well, when we left the lawyers office, my sister promised to take good care of her. I was told by my doctor that I would feel like a burden was lifted off of my shoulders, but I sure didn't feel that way. My heart was full of emptiness.

Now I started going out every night feeling sorry for myself that I had failed in everything. Soon I met a nice guy that could dance real good. We started going out a lot and got to know each other pretty well. It seemed like fun at first, but he started mistreating me and using me. He took my car while I was at work and took other girls out as he was not employed. At first he would come over and pick me up from work but then it got so that I had to catch the bus home from work. I would then call the bar where he hung out and they said that he had left so I would catch another bus to the bar and when I got there he would say that he had some business to take care of and that beings that my mother didn't want him around was why he didn't come to get me at home. The reason mother didn't like him was because he was still married. Of course he told mother that he was separated and intended to stay with me until the divorce and we would probably get married. I guess mother could see something that I couldn't as she didn't believe him. With the way that mother felt I decided that I would stay with him where ever he lived.

He didn't have a place to call his own. Different guys would let him stay at their place until they found out that he wouldn't pay rent and would kick him out. I wanted so bad to have a man to call my own that I did whatever he wanted. I would stay out all night with him, sometimes at the place where he lived at the time or we would rent a motel. Of course, I paid for it as he had no money or a job. I did this as I wanted to be wanted so bad and thought that he wanted me and believed that he would find a job. I also wanted to show my mother that I intended to do what I wanted to do and didn't have to answer to her anymore as I was grown up now. This was only making things worse. Sometimes this guy would tell me to go home and stay to make my mother happy I would, but later I found out why as he would keep my car to sleep in. I found this out from my friends. So I told him that I had heard that he was sleeping in my car and that wasn't right. So I suggested to get an apartment. He went for this. I paid for it all. Now I was in debt again. As time went on he started doing the same things to me again only worse. He was bringing girls into the apartment while I was at work. He had gotten a job but had quit it again. I told him that I was moving back home and he agreed that we(ha) couldn't afford it. I told him that I was breaking up with him and would see him around at the bar. Little did I know what I was in store for. I stayed away from the bar for a while and finally went back one night for a drink. He came over and said that he realized what he had done and wanted to go back with me. I accepted and it was back to the same old thing again. He kept my car and took girls out through the day. When I found out this time I took action. I took my car away from him the next evening when I met him at the bar. I asked a couple of friends to go to Maryland to a dance place with me and they agreed. When we got there my ex boyfriend was there with the waitress from the bar that we had just left. My friends told me that that was the one that he had been taking out in my car. Well, I was furious and proceeded to get good and drunk.

My friends told me that they would ride back with someone else as they didn't want to get involved with what I had planned to do. I planned to meet both of them (my ex and his girl) in the parking lot. I left the bar and got a bottle to go and sat outside in my car. Finally, out they came and I sat there watching. My ex boyfriend came over and asked me if I wanted to have a drink with them over in the car they were sitting in and I told him no way that I wanted to talk to her. She came over and I told her that I wanted a piece of her you know what. I through my glasses into my car and jumped out and knocked her down to the ground and sat on her. She was twice my size. I was so violent at her that I just kept beating her in the face. Everyone finally pulled me off of her. She started crying and saying that she wanted to be my friend as she had no friends. I calmed down and felt sorry for her. Again I was made a fool of by both of them. I agreed to take her back to Virginia and get her a place to stay in a motel for the night as she had no place to stay. She had gotten fired from her job that night. I believed my ex boyfriend that we would leave her there and go our merry way. It didn't happen that way. When we got to the motel she took a shower while I sat and had a drink and when she came out he went to take a shower and when he came out he climbed in bed with her and told me to go home. I was furious by now and he kicked me out and told me to go home and he would see me tomorrow. I left but with revenge. I didn't go to work the next day, I slept in my car and went to the bar the following morning.

Everyone complimented me for what I had done. Little did they know what really happened after the fight. I told them about it. While I was sitting there the two drove up and came into the bar, the owner told them that they were barred and could not come in. Well, for some reason my friends knew more about him then I did and told me to go out and get my registration out of my car because if he tried to steal my car I could call the police and have him locked up for stealing. Sure enough he took my car and I called the police we chased him around town and he brought the car right back to the bar. The police asked him for the registration and he couldn't find it in the glove compartment. The police asked if I wanted to press charges and I told him no that I just wanted him to leave me alone and the police told him to leave me alone of the next time he would lock him up.

I went back into the bar and while I was setting there we heard a crash noise and looked out to see my ex boyfriend throwing my car radio up against the wall and breaking it into bits and pieces. I said well enough as he had put the radio in the car for me anyway and I would get another one. I went back into the bar and forgot about it. Later on everyone decided to go downtown to this dance hall and I went along. We were sitting there and in came my ex boyfriend, I told everyone that I was afraid of him and they said don't worry that they would take care of him if he touched me.

I was sitting there and everyone was up dancing, he walked by me and went behind me to go to the men's room when he came out he came up behind me and slapped his hands on my glasses and broke them in pieces, I couldn't see what happened from then on but everyone told me that three other guys chased him and caught him and held him until the police got there. They locked him up. I put on my prescription sunglasses so that I could see and drove home after the dance. Little did I know that the police let him out of jail. I noticed that someone was following me, but had no idea that it was him. He had borrowed someone's car and was trying to run me off of the road. I turned around and ran every red light back to the police headquarters and ran in and told them what happened. They followed me home and found him hiding around the corner of the police station and locked him up until the court date the next day. In court they let him off providing that he left town and went back to his wife. He did just that and we never saw him again. Thank God.

CHAPTER 6

Trying to Do the Right Thing

A few months past and I found out that I was pregnant. I told mother and she was very upset. She told me that I would have to leave home as it would be too embarrassing for her to go through this again. I talked to a few friends and they said that I could move in with them. I left home and started going to the doctors. I also had to quit my job. Where I was living I was their maid and babysitter. That is what I did until I got very sick one night and they took me to the hospital and found out that I was losing my baby. I must say that it was God's way of warning me and they finally did the abortion and I was out of the hospital the next day. This didn't stop my drinking or partying. I was looking for a job again. I still hadn't found a job and the woman that was letting me stay there told me that I had to move soon. I went to the bar to have a drink and talk to my friend that owned the bar and low and behold in walked my old boyfriend, Sue's father, he motioned for me to come over. I was afraid but did talk to him the first thing he said was why did you let your sister adopt my baby. He said that he wanted her if I didn't. I got so mad that I told him to get out. I said that he didn't want her four years ago and forget me and her. We exchanged a few bad words and he left. I cried when he walked out because I was so confused by now that I actually thought that I was going crazy like everyone said. I think at this point it shows the insanity of alcohol and drugs.

I felt so depressed that I didn't want to live. I stayed until the place closed and really didn't want to go home. I didn't want to talk to my mother about this as she would not understand how I felt, I thought. So I went to Maryland with some friends and drank myself sick. When it was time to go home I just drove around until I got tired and stopped down on the boulevard and cried myself to sleep and woke up at sunrise in my car. I felt sick and depressed and didn't want to go to work so I went to the bar again. Finally, everyone convinced me to call my mother and work and I did. I went home around noon and mother didn't say much so I told her that I couldn't go on feeling this way. I went to the doctor and told him about it and he suggested that I get away from everything that was bothering me which meant my mother, sister, work and especially my bill collectors.

So first I went into work and told them that I was going to quit as I was leaving town. I did that and drew out my retirement. I went home and laid around a few days and mother told me to get out. I really felt like committing suicide but was too afraid to. I packed a suitcase and left telling mother that I would be back for the rest of my things. I went to the bar and ran into some of my friends and told them what I did. I stayed with the owner that night. She and her husband introduced me to a real nice guy that was old enough to be my father. He had a lot of money and said that he would help me get a place with no strings attached and believe me it was just that way. I sold my old car as it was broken down anyway. This man talked me into going back home and mother accepted me when she saw how nice he was. She liked him. He talked with her for a while and said that he would help me get straightened out. Well, he took me lots of places and treated me like a queen, but I didn't like him. He bought me a car and gave me money for nothing. He told me that he loved me and that was why he was doing this. I finally told him that I couldn't let this go on any longer as I couldn't hurt him. By now I had gotten a job back with the government. So I stopped seeing him and started back to the old bar that I used to hang out. I kept a low profile this time and acted with respect for myself. I came alone and left alone. One day there was a guy that kept send-ing me over drinks. I told the waitress to tell him to stop but he wouldn't. That night a girlfriend and I were going over to Maryland after the bar closed. This guy kept trying to talk to me and asked me out after the bar closed. I kept resist-ing but finally accepted when his friend asked my girlfriend out too. So we told them that we were going to the Moose Lodge and for them to meet us there.

We walked outside and noticed that these guys had a new car. The one that wanted to take me out walked over and asked what we wanted to drink as they were going across the bridge to get a bottle and we both told them what we liked. Then they asked us if we wanted to ride over with them and we agreed. We went to the Moose and had a real nice time. This guy named Joe was so nice to me, he told me that he was looking for a real nice girl as he was getting a divorce and needed a companion. I backed off right away. I actually told him that I had been through too many heart aches to fool with a guy again that was married. He begged to see me again and of course I agreed. I really liked his approach. Well, he took me back to my car and asked to see me again the next night. I accepted. He called me at work and told me he would call me later at home and tell me what time he would pick me up. He did and met mother and mother just fell in love with him after talking to her. He told her that he knew what all I had been through and that he thought that we were made for each other.

I was so happy that night. He took me to some real nice places and brought me home early enough and told me he would see me again. He called me the next day and picked me up after work. We started going out steady. We went out for months without having any sex and until one night I asked him why he didn't try and he said that when he had heard about my past that he didn't want to push me. Well, of course that worked just fine with me and from then on we became very close and intimate. Before long I was pregnant. I was terrified when I told him. He said not to worry and told me in the same breath that he was not divorced yet but was waiting to catch her in an act with this other man. I found out that he was telling the truth but I still told him that I was going to get an abortion and he said no way that we would have this baby. He said that we would go home and tell my mother that we planned to get married the following weekend and go and rent an apartment and for me to keep the baby. I felt on cloud nine.

Well, the following weekend we had already gotten the apartment and pretended to get married for mothers sake as he wasn't divorced yet. The apartment was furnished and I was so happy but he only stayed with me until around 11PM everynite and went home to his wife's house. I cried every nite he left but ie always returned the next day as soon as I got home from work. I changed my name at work so I could stay on. I accepted this and we had so much fun together. We went everywhere together. I as so happy. I knew that he would marry me some day. I had a wonderful job too. They let me work right up to the end about one week before my baby was born. We had a baby girl. Things started happening near the last month between us as he would stay at the bar and come late and leave me alone. The couple that owned the bar told me to call them if I needed them. Welll, thank God he was with me when my water broke but I panicked so I called my friend and she came over right away. It wasn't time for me to go to the hospital yet and Joe told me that he had to go to work as I wasn't going to have the babyh until later just like the doctor told me and he went on to work. This hurt me and I me and I was also afraid to be alone, my friend told me also that she had to go and open the store up and that she would get someone to come and stay with me until it was time to go. She got one of our old friends, a real old man, I didn't like this but it had to do. Finally, my pain got closer together and I told him, lets go to the hospital. I was so embarrassed going to the hospital with him. I made sure that I told them at the hospital that my husband was at work and that he was just a friend. They checked me in and I had the baby 12 hours later. My husband came in later that nite and saw the baby and me. We had a baby girl. We were so happy. When the third day came it was time to take the baby and go home. My husband told me that he wouldn't be able to take me home and asked my mother to come and get me. My sister and mother came to get me and took me home. They stayed with me for a while and left. I waited for Joe to show up. He didn't come and it was getting dark and there I was all alone with the baby. I called around to find him and no one knew where he was. I was crying so bad that the lady down stairs came up to talk to me. She said why don't you go and try to find him and I will take care of the baby for you. I got dressed and went to the bar where Joe goes, up the street. They said Joe had been in but didn't know where that he went. I found that he had just left. I finally get someone to tell me where he had gone and they that he had gone to North Beach, MD. I went back to the apartment and called some friends and they agreed to take me to the beach to find him. My friend that lived downstairs said that she would take care of the baby for me. The beach wasn't too far away. When I got there and walked into one of the bars everyone looked shocked to see me. They asked me how the baby was and I kept asking where was Joe. I told them that I knew that Joe was there and to tell me where he was. Finally, they told me where he was. I walked over to the motel where he was partying with these other people with the door wide open. They were laying around drinking. I walked in and said thanks for being there when the baby and I came home. We went round and round and finally when he found out that the baby was alright he got me a drink and told me to calm down. I asked him why he was with those people partying and he told me that it wasn't what I thought that it was a big mixed party and nothing was going on . He was surprised that the guy that showed me where he was happened to be Sue's father, my other daughter's father. Joe had become good friends with him.

That night The partying got rough and I asked Joe to take me home and he said for me to go home and take care of the baby. I was so humiliated and hurt I ran back to the restaurant to find someone to take me back home. Sue's dad took me home. When I got home I told my friend what happened and she said he'll come home and will have sowed-his-oats and will settle down. She told me that some men do that when their woman gets pregnant. She was right he came home the next day. I was so hurt and upset that night as I thought that it was going to be the same thing all over again as it was when I had Sue. He apologized, saying that he was throwing his last fling. I believed him. From then on he was being exceptionally good to me and the baby.

The new house was nice. We seemed to be getting along much better. I had money to buy things I wanted to fix the house up and enjoyed it. This soon got old and I wanted to go out with

Joe. As usual he stayed out at the bars and got drunk and I stayed home and got drunk. Tracy was in school by now by the way which gave me a lot of time during the day to go out and drink with some of my friends I met back in town. It got so that I was racing home to pick up Tracy at school and finally asking my next door neighbor picking her up from school and me just getting home in time to cook dinner for Joe. I was always wasted. We started going camping a lot and ended up buying a trailer to go camping in. We had all of the nice things to enjoy life but still drinking was interfering with everything. We still were fighting and arguing. Somehow we kept thinking that our problems were normal and coped with it. I really learned to cope as I loved being able to go and come as I pleased and didn't mind Joe staying out at the bar. I told him that I would keep the car at home and go where I wanted to and he rode with the buddies that he drank with. It worked fine as we stayed clear of each other. Little did we know that we were becoming strangers to each other. We decided to take the camper for the summer and leave it on the camp site and he commuted back and forth to work leaving Tracy and I at the campsite to have fun.

I enjoyed it at first as there were other families doing the same thing. Tracy got to meet new playmates and I met new friends as well. We stayed there for three months. I wasn't enjoying the cooking part of it as Joe wanted a full course meal every night and this was hard to do camping out. Everyone told him he was crazy as it put a burden on me to cook. He said that I had all day to play and it didn't hurt to cook one meal a day for him as he was working all day. I agreed, but resented it. I had forgot that I had entered Tracy in to a beauty contest so I kept the car one day and went back home to get her all prettied up for the contest. There were hundreds of other entries. Tracy didn't win. I think she would have won as she passed every test except the verbal one. The judges said that she must have had stage fright as she just stood there looking at them and wouldn't talk. I told them that that had to be true as usually her mouth ran constantly. So we left there and went back to the camp site. She was also upset as when we went home to change clothes we found that her birds had died. Her dad was supposed to go home and feed them each day before he came to the camp site. Maybe she was upset over that. Her dad was very upset that she didn't win the contest. I told him when hundreds of kids enter its hard to pick just one. But he had no feelings and made her feel badly about not winning. I told her to ignore him. Everyone else at the camp site told her that she was a winner in their book, and this made her feel better. Soon she got over it.

CHAPTER 7

Turning Point

The summer was over and it was time to go back home. We got settled back into winter and soon the holidays were here. There were lots of parties and we didn't miss one of them. One night we were coming home from a party and we were both smashed. The roads were icy and slippery. He was relying on my judgment as to where to turn and I told him that I couldn't see as the windows were frosted over. When he turned onto the road, which was under construction before it snowed, it ended up being the parking lot that they hadn't finished and suddenly the car just dropped down, we hit a barrel which rolled onto the car, luckily it didn't break the windshield, it then rolled over the top of the car and somehow we kept going and got back onto the road. Thank God there were lice that time of the morning. The next thing steam started rolling out from the front of the car and it was the radiator, it had gotten damaged when we hit the barrel. We had to park the car and we were about 2 miles from home. He got mad at me and said that it was all my fault. We started walking as there were no cabs to be found. I kept slipping and we both staggered but he kept kicking me and cussing me all the way home. When we got home he beat me and the only way that he stopped was that I told him that I was going to call the police again. He then apologized.

We slept off the drunk and went down to get the car fixed and picked up Tracy. The rest of the day went pretty well. We had invited people over to our house for a party. Everyone got drunk and some went home and some stayed. When I woke up the next morning people were sleeping everywhere and the house was a total mess. Joe got up and everyone else suggested going out to get another drink. Everyone went but me, Joe said that I had to stay home and take care of Tracy. I didn't like this but I did cope with it. I cleaned the house and waited for Joe to return.

Nighttime came and he didn't come home I called everywhere I knew he could be and no one knew. I got worried and called his boss's daughter's house, she lived near us. She said that Joe was there and that he had been locked up and was upset. She said that this was why he didn't come home first. What happened was that when he left the bar, the owner took his keys and told him to lay down in his car and sleep off the drunk before he drove home. What actually happened was Joe woke up and went back into the bar and raised a ruckus and finally the owner gave him his keys back and Joe drove off the parking lot and ran into a police car, and then balled out the policeman for hitting him. Joe got a lawyer who suggested that with all the past problems that Joe had had in court with drinking problems that he had better go to AA and when he came to court they would go a bit lighter on him for trying to correct his drinking problem.

So Joe came home and started going to AA the next night. After a few meetings, he asked me to go with him. I rebelled and said that I didn't have any problems. Little did I know that I did, but didn't want to admit it. I was still able to function, so I thought. I continued to drink but I hid it in a colored glass so that it would not tempt him. He knew that I was drinking and kept after me until I finally agreed to go to the Al-Anon meetings. Well, this certainly didn't help me, since I thought it was boring. Little did I know that this was the beginning of the end of our relationship. Joe stayed sober for three months and went to court and his case was suspended. Soon after this, he started back drinking.

Joe's job was becoming a safety problem and he said that he didn't want to work there any-more. He asked me if I wanted to go back to VA and, of course I said yes. He told me to pack enough clothes for Tracy and I for about two weeks and they had an overtime job in VA that he wanted to make some extra money as well as check up and see if there was any job openings in VA. When we got to VA, we stayed at moth-ers for the weekend and found a house to live in. He also found a good job. The following Friday night, I put him on a plane and he went back to

Connecticut and rented a truck and drove all our belongings back to VA. We moved in the following weekend.

It was nice to be back home. But the happiness soon wore off. Joe and I were back drinking heavy again and arguing and fighting. Not only were we having problems but his ex wife called and said that the boys needed their teeth fixed and for Joe to take them until their teeth got fixed as the insurance on his job covered the dental work. We agreed and I was back to playing Mom again. This time the younger boy rebelled just like before, but every time I told Joe about it, he would get on my case in front of the boy and this made it very difficult for me when he wasn't around.

Off and on I was getting beat up by Joe two or three times a week and each time he would blame it on my drinking. He told me that I could not come to the bar anymore as my place was at home raising the children and when my daughter was 18 years old then and only then, could I run out to the bar. Well, this made me furious and I turned on the boys as well as him. Finally, one evening I called him at the bar and told him that I was coming and got a babysitter. This was bad but I felt that people in the bar had a right to know what a no good guy he was. When I got there, he seemed in a good mood, but I wasn't. I proceeded to tell everyone about our problems and he said if I didn't like it to leave him. I said fine and one thing led to another. We got into a heavy fight and it ended up in the parking lot. There in front of everyone he beat me so bad that he broke my nose. Blood was flying everywhere. I didn't know that my nose was broken at the time. He kept trying to get me in the car and I kept wiping the blood all over his car. Finally, he got me into the car and took me home. My nose wouldn't stop bleeding. I told him to take me to the hospital and he refused as he said that they would lock him up.

When I got home, the children asked what happened and he told them that we got into a fight. I told him that I was going to call my mother and take Tracy and leave and also go to the police. He begged me not to go and cried saying that he would never do it again. Again, like a fool, I did nothing. I stayed in the house for weeks and he was good to me. Both of my eyes were black and my nose didn't see too bad. So stupid of me to let another incident go by.

About a week later I started having female problems, the doctor told me that I had to stop taking the pill or I would bleed to death. I went into the hospital for a minor surgery. I then told the doctor that I did not want any more children and want a tubligation. He told me that my husband

and I both had to sign a letter stating that we both agreed to do this. No problem, Joe signed with no questions. It was set up for two weeks away. Two days before I was to go into the hospital for my surgery, Joe up and took the two boys and left. He took the trailer that we had and disappeared. I figured that I would outwit him and called a storage company and had all the furniture and clothes, except two weeks of clothing for Tracy and I, put in storage.

The next day I stayed with a friend and watched the apartment to see if Joe would return. Sure enough, Joe came back and everything was gone. Tracy and I stayed with mother until I had the operation. Joe came to the hospital to see me and asked why I put everything in storage, I told him that he would never get anything and to leave me alone.

After the operation I got back on my feet trying to find a job but couldn't. I started going out looking for Joe as well as boozing it up looking for some friends. I was so hurt and depressed. I felt like I was all alone in this cruel world. Mother understood my problem for a while but it became a nightmare in one week. It was almost an instant replay, except with a different child, Tracy. She kept telling me that she was going to see to it that Tracy was taken away from me. This time I acted quickly.

I called a friend in Connecticut and told her happened and she said she was glad I got away from him. She told me to come back up there and get a job. She had a place for Tracy and I to stay. I was drinking heavy now, but was determined that Joe would never see Tracy or me again and made the drastic decision to go to Connecticut. I found a couple that offered to drive us to Connecticut.

Once again we bid our goodbyes to all and took off for Connecticut. When we got there everyone was happy to see us. The next day I was very depressed. I went down to apply for different jobs and there had been a bad storm and all of the buses were on strike as well. Nothing but obstacles everywhere I went. So I went on welfare. This was the worst thing I could have ever done. My girlfriend lived on the first floor and I lived on the third. Her live-in boyfriend did not like me to drink with her. She also had a drinking problem and was on welfare, but this boyfriend of hers lived there and helped out with the finances, so what he said was law.

He blamed me for her drinking so I had to make sure that I was not seen near her. Now I really was alone. I met another friend next door who also was on welfare. Her kids were Tracy's age and went to the same school. I spent a lot of time with this new friend. I met some bad people through her. I was drinking so much that I didn't know what was going on most of the time. This woman knew of my problems and used me. It was very convenient as I paid her for watching Tracy while I went out and drank. Finally, I decided that I had better get myself together. I started staying in my apartment.

It became my prison, little did I know at the time. Tracy told me that I would pass out and would wake me up later knowing my pattern that I would be shaking badly and need a drink, which she would run across to the corner store and tell them to send up some beer. The corner store was my drug store. It was the only real world I knew at this time. I ran a tab for food and beer. The only food bought on the tab was for Tracy. I was at the point where I was too sick to eat. If I tried to eat I would get violently sick. I would pay on my bill when I got my check each month. It was a never ending debt.

I also conned men I met into buying me a bottle. My pantry was full of booze. Somehow I managed to get a phone installed. I had become an outcast to my friend that lived on the first floor. She tried to straighten me out but I told her to bug off. I was letting minors come up and drink in my flat. One day I was sitting in my apartment watching TV with Tracy having a few drinks when someone knocked on the door, it was a guy I knew of but he was a trouble maker. It was the end of the month and I had just cashed my check. I was afraid that if he came in that he might steal my money. I told him to go away and he pushed his way in. I told him that he could have one drink and that he had to go. I had to go into the kitchen for something and told Tracy to watch out for my purse. When I came back Tracy said that this guy had gotten into my purse and stolen my wallet and ran.

I called the police and somehow to this day I do not know how I got locked up but they threw me into the police car and locked me up. My friend took care of Tracy. The police told me that they would let me out on my own so I caught a cab home and asked the cab to wait while I ran to get the money to pay him. When I got back down stairs to pay him the police were there and told me that the cab driver called them saying that I skipped off without paying him I tried to tell them that I ran upstairs to get my money and they wouldn't listen they literally threw me into the patty wagon. The next morning in jail I woke up without my glasses and my face and arms were bruised from the police beating me. When it went to court that morning the judge threw the case out of court. I wanted to sue them for beating me but I wasn't sure what happened and by this time, I was afraid of the police. I found out through the grapevine that the reason the police beat me around because I was letting minors into my apartment. This was just one of my misfortunes.

I sort of straightened my act up. No one was allowed in my apartment. There was a guy who worked for the Tree Surgeon Company next door that took a liking to Tracy and me. He knew of my misfortune and sort of stayed close to protect us. I didn't like him for a boyfriend and told him so but lucky for me he came along as I'm sure it was a matter of time before I would have ended up a basket case. He took us out to eat sometimes and of course all I did was drink. By now my appetite was little or nothing. Booze was my food. This guy also kept me in booze. My friend downstairs moved out. She came up and asked me if I wanted to become the resident manager as the owner needed a replacement. This sounded good as I would get my rent free and have it made financially. So I became the resident manager. I collected all the rent and kept it for the owner to pick up. This made a change in my attitude towards life and I started to attempt to changing my life. At least respecting myself and Tracy.

One day I got a call from my mother stating that I had gotten a notice that all of my furniture in storage as well as my personal belongings were going to be put up for auction and furthermore, if I showed up on the premises that I would be locked up. I tried to get in touch with the company and they refused to talk to me. They just told me that my belongings had been in storage for one year and they hadn't heard from me so they were putting it up for auction.

By now my drinking was an obsession and I was having blackouts quite a bit. I had no idea what day and time it was. All I did was exist. Of course, hearing about losing my belongings made things worse so I drank from sun rise to sunset. Loosing my personal belongings was a good reason for me to stay drunk. I felt that there was nothing to live for now and didn't care. To this day I believe that hadn't I had my daughter with me then that I would have drank myself to death. Soon I accepted that I had lost everything but happy that Joe didn't get the furniture. Still I had defeated my whole purpose, but nevertheless, I still had Tracy and was happy, I thought.

Physical problems started to surface. I developed pleurisy and a blood clot in my left lung. This was found out when one day I woke up and could not breathe without a sharp pain in my chest. I was rushed to the hospital and they removed the fluid from my lungs as well as dissolved the blood clot that had traveled to my lung. They actually saved my life. I was put on a medication that was to regulate my blood back to normal, as when they dissolved the blood clot they had to thin my blood. I stayed in the hospital for about 3 weeks and when I was released I still had to be checked everyday to see if my blood was returning to normal. No one told me that I could not drink while taking the medicine. So I continued my drinking just as heavy as before. One week later I got deathly sick again and went to another doctor. When he found out that I was taking this medicine for my blood and drinking he was hysterical and told me to discontinue the medication as I could kill myself drinking with that certain type of medicine. I did so and everything was okay.

By now I was very depressed and started realizing that I could no longer control my drinking and needed to find help. The only help that I was looking for was someone to take care of Tracy. I tried to find Joe and had no success. I was afraid that I would lose Tracy to the state if I didn't find help. I stayed depressed day and night. I felt so alone and Tracy tried to make me happy. She doctored me when I got sick and managed to have booze sent in when she figured I needed it to survive. Even though she was only 8 years old, she seemed to handle me as though she was my mother. It was totally confusing by now.

One day my sister called and told me that mother had cancer and that the doctor wanted to see her and I both as soon as possible to decide whether to tell mother about the cancer or not. I told my sister that I would be there as soon as possible. I didn't have much money so Tracy and I had to take the bus home. I was happy in a way that I was going home, but not was hoping that it was all a dream that mother had cancer.

Tracy and I packed a few things and, of course, I packed a fifth of booze and carried a small bottle in my purse to make it home on the bus. We had to transfer in new York. When we got to NY, I had drank all my booze. I managed to get a few beers near the station and got on the next bus heading for home. I started to get the shakes and Tracey noticed that some young college kids were drinking in the back of the bus, so she went back and told them that I needed a drink without telling me and one of them came up and asked if I wanted a drink. I found out Tracy had told them my problem.

Well, we arrived in Washington, DC and my sister was there to greet us. We went straight to the hospital to see mother, and I was so happy to se her, that I cried. Mother asked why I was there and I told her that I was planning on coming back to Virginia to live. We didn't want her to think that I was there because of her problem. My sister and I went down to the cafeteria to get something to eat, and I told her I wasn't hungry but needed a drink. She said to eat something. We sat down and I told her that I felt like I was going to faint. She said let's go home and I could rest for awhile before we went to go see the doctor.

When we got home, I had a beer and changed clothes and off we went to see my mother's doctor. We made a decision not to tell mother that she had cancer, but the doctor said that mother didn't have long to live as the cancer had traveled all through her body. When we left the doctor's, I told my sister that I needed a drink badly and went home. When we got there, I sat down on the couch and she got me another beer. The next thing I knew I was laying on the floor and there were men in dark suits standing over me asking me questions. They took me to the hospital. The doctor's told me I had had a seizure.

My sister and Tracy told me that I took a sip of beer and my head went back, I stiffened out and kicked the coffee table over and dropped the beer. My eyes rolled back in my head and I was making funny noises and moaning. She said that it scared her and Tracy to death. Later on that evening, I was sitting in the living room and the phone rang. It was for me, and it was from Connecticut, and all I remember was answering the phone and come to at the hospital again.

This time, they said that I had a grand mal seizure. My heart stopped beating for awhile, and it took me about an hour to tell them who I was and where I lived.

They gave me some medicine to take for the seizures so I wouldn't have another one and said that I was malnutrition and to eat more food. My sister and brother-in-law talked me into staying in Virginia. I didn't have any more seizures, but went to see their doctor and he told me that what I had was an alcoholic seizure. Meaning, that I was hooked on alcohol and when I stopped drinking for a period of time that my body would go into shock and the seizures would continue until I decided to get detoxed. After I left his office, I realized that if I wanted to continue to drink, that I had to drink all the time, so I didn't have another seizure. Of course it didn't enter my mind to quit. I thought I was having too much fun drinking. Also, I really didn't believe him about getting detox. I just made sure that I had something to drink all the time. The doctor gave me tranquilizers to take and also the medicine so that I wouldn't have any more seizures and left it up to me to get help or go get detox.

I stayed with my sister until I could find a job and apartment for Tracy and I to live. Living with my sister was the pits. She treated me like a kid and Tracy felt mistreated. We lived in the basement of her house until I found a job. I felt that I was a prisoner there. With all my drinking and problems, I finally found a job with the help of my brother-in-law back in the government. By me going to work, they loaned me some money to make it until I got my first paycheck. Most of it was going to booze. Now my sister was on me for drinking too much and we were fighting a lot. So to avoid the arguments, I decided to scheme a plan.

You see, my sister and brother-in-law drank heavy too, but they denied it when I confronted them. The only way that they didn't develop the same problems that I did, was because they had plenty of money to keep their supply on hand all of the time. When my sister and I went grocery shopping, she stopped every day and get two gallon of booze about twice a week. Also, they would argue about how much booze was missing and how much each other was drinking it. My sister would accuse my brother-in-law of drinking too much, and truthfully, he seemed to show it more than she did, so to avoid her criticism, he would go to bed early. My sister and I would sit up and drink a few more hours before retiring to bed.

Soon my old drinking mind got a plan set in motion. I discovered where they hid their bottles in the house. I figured that if I proved to them that I wasn't spending my money on booze that things would be a little bit easier to live there. So I kept a few empty bottles in the basement and when they would go out of the house, I would go to their hiding places and sipher booze from each bottle. Finally, I had myself a good stock in the basement. They didn't know I had taken it. Although I would hear them accusing each other of drinking too much, but what did I care? I was safe in the basement and had all I needed. This went on for a long time, and I started drinking it like it was medicine. I carried a small bottle to work with me and went to the bathroom and drank a little every four hours just to keep the shakes from coming on. I didn't want my boss to know that I had this problem.

The time had come for Tracy and I to find an apartment. We found one in Alexandria. I had to rent by the week and thought this was great. My sister gave me some furniture to start with and now Tracy and I were alone. I found a babysitter that was real nice. She had a little girl that liked Tracy, and was in Tracy's class. This worked out good as I would walk Tracy every morning down to her apartment and catch the bus to work on the corner in front of her apartment. Ritually my routine every morning would be get Tracy up and dressed for school and fill my bottle with booze for work, walk Tracy to the babysitter's and head for work. On my way home, I would stop everyday and buy two bottles of booze to last. I never wanted to run out of booze.

I found myself sometimes in the evenings waking up on the couch and had no idea where Tracy was. I would find her next door or outside. This started to scare me. I knew that I was passing out by was afraid to tell anyone. I talked to my neighbor who was an old lady and she said she would keep an eye out for Tracy, but that I should seriously think of getting help for myself. I told her that I would. Eventually, I became so paranoid that I began to find Tracy's Dad.

I called the local that he worked out of and they took my name and said that if they could locate him, they would have him call. I told them that it was an emergency and needed help as I was very sick and needed him to take Tracy to care for. Of course, I got no answer.

Tracy was going to Sunday school and becoming involved. I told her to tell the preacher to come and talk to me, that I needed help. She brought him home one Sunday. I told him that I had a drinking problem and needed help so I could go and get detox. He told me that he would take Tracy home with him and not to worry. Tracy agreed to go with him and little did I know that this was the beginning of a horrible nightmare. Now Tracy was gone and I was all alone. I remember getting dressed and leaving the apartment. I went back tot the area where my mother and I used to live to a bar and ran into some people I knew. I told them what Joe had done and where Tracy was and that I was trying to get my life together.

Now is where the horror story begins. I cannot remember what really happened from that day on exactly, but it's just horrible trying to remember parts of it to tell you. I am going to tell you what I have been able to remember with the help of flash backs that I have had from time to time.

Before Tracy went to the preacher, a lot happened to me, which caused me to make my decision. Mother was progressively getting worse. She went back into the hospital. My sister stayed at the hospital every day with her and would call me at work and tell me how mother was doing. On April Fool's Day, my sister called me and said that mother is not expected to make it through the day, but not to come because she didn't want me to miss any more work. I told her that I was coming no matter what. My boss was mad with me, as I had been taking a lot of time off from work and didn't have leave built up. I didn't care, I wanted to see my mother.

I told the girl at my office that I was leaving to go to the hospital to see my mother before she died.

I called a friend that had a car to come pick me up and was standing out front waiting on her to show up when my boss came walking out and asked where I was going. I told him that my sister had called and said that my mother was dying and I was going to the hospital. He said that I didn't have any leave and that he would dock my pay. I was so hurt and mad that he could do whatever he had too, and that I was going to quit anyways. He told me that I would receive a letter of reprimand. When my friend came, I told her what he said and I cried all the way to the hospital.

When I got to the hospital, my mother knew who I was, but was failing fast. I held her hand and stayed by her bed until she died. She died shortly after I arrived. My sister and I went crazy. They gave me a sedative, on top of the booze we had been drinking, and I felt totally numb. I vaguely remember leaving the hospital. Somehow, I must of blacked out again, from all the drugs. I do remember going by and buying a bottle and going to the babysitters to pick up Tracy.

When I told Tracy that Grandmother had died she thought I was telling a joke as it was April Fool's Day, until I started crying and told her that was the reason I was so late. Tracy and I both went home crying. I went to my sisters the next day. Tracy and I stayed there for the funeral. I know that I was totally out at the funeral. I can vaguely remember it, I do remember Tracy crying unbearably over her death at the funeral home. Someone took her and held her, as I couldn't control her. After the funeral, Tracy and I went home and just sat around feeling depressed. My work called and asked me if I was coming in and I told them off and said I would be in to get my personal belongings and resign. Shortly, after I resigned, I realized what had been done and asked the preacher to take Tracy.

Now that I was all alone, I went to bars looking for someone that could help me find Joe. I ran into a guy that knew him and said that he would help me. He took me home that night, and when I got there my apartment had a lock on it. I couldn't get in. This guy felt sorry for me and put me up in a hotel room for the night, and gave me some money and said that he would be back the next day to help me find Joe and get my apartment straightened out.

Well, he never showed up and when I talked to the people at the apartment project they said I was past due on my rent for two weeks and I couldn't get my things until I paid them. I went back to the bar for help again, as now I was really all alone. Now I had no place to live and no money or even a job. I hopped from bar to bar trying to get help. I ran into a guy who told me he would help until I got a job so I went with him. We went riding down to the country where this woman would let men alcoholics come and dry out while they worked for her. When she saw that I was there, she said that I had to leave as it was only for men. She did say that I could live in one of her rooming houses in Alexandria and for him to take me there. One the way back, we drank quite a bit and when we got to the rooming house, he literally kicked me out of the car. I fell on the sidewalk and all I had on was a bathing suit and a beach coat. I had no idea where my other clothes were. My knees were cut badly and I was hurting all over. I was afraid the police would pick me up and put me in jail.

It was early in the morning, somewhere around 1:00 am. I went and sat down on the porch of the rooming house. I had no idea of where I was going or what to do. I just sat there like a small child and cried. Evidently, I must of have been pretty loud as some man that lived in the rooming house came out and asked what was wrong. I told him what happening and he took me to his room. I told him that the lady that owned the rooming house told me I could stay there, but she was still down in the country. He told me that I could stay in his room, as he had to go to work and not to worry, that she should be back to Alexandria the next day. Well, she did come back. In the meantime, I met all of the other roomers. I met this real old man across the hall. He was sitting there with his door open drinking a beer and told me to come in and have a beer. I told him my life history just about and he said that he had some money to give me to go down the street and buy an outfit. I thanked him and did just that. When I got back, he had a bottle and a case of beer. Well, that's all I needed to be happy so I proceeded to get drunk as I felt that I was among friends. I guess you could say I was, because all that lived in that house was drunks.

In the meantime, the lady showed up and told me to stay with the old man and not the other guy, as she trusted me staying with him rather than a younger man. She told me that this was only a temporary thing and she would try and find me help. I can't begin to tell you how these people lived. They never ate. There was a kitchen downstairs but no one ever cooked. The old man and I would cook soup on his hot plate. He had emphysema and was a retired roofer. Lots of people came to visit him. He understood that I had the shakes and tried to help me break my drinking habit, but as people come to visit they brought something to drink and by evening we were all drunk again.

The lady was upset that I was not trying to better myself. One day she brought this nice looking man dressed up in a suit to meet me and he told me that he had just come from detox, and would take me away from that environment. After talking to him, I found out that he knew my sister from high school. He asked me if I wanted to go and live with him in his apartment and maybe think about getting detox also. I said yes. After we got into the car he told me that he needed someone to drive his car as he had lost his driving license. He had a job but had gotten hurt on the job and was collecting compensation. He was a maintenance man and had burned his leg very badly.

He bought me some clothes and in turn I kept his apartment clean and took care of changing his bandages on his leg. He had to go to the doctors twice a week to have it checked and I would drive him there. I told him about losing my daughter and some of my past. He told me that he would help me get straight and get my daughter back. I sat down that night and told him just what had been happening to me in the past. I told him about my blackouts and hours disappearing from my memory. How I'd wake up in bed with strangers. Each time I would promise myself that it would never happen again, but it did happen again, time and time again. I stopped promising it would never happen again and instead I would have another drink trying to ignore my "death". I was consciously aware that I was dying as a person. I didn't recognize whoever I was becoming, but I couldn't stop it. I remember the agony of waking up mornings after drinking myself into an oblivion and I'd pray with my eyes still closed that this was my bed I was in. Alone. If it was, I drank in relief, if it wasn't I'd drink in desperate pain. The only thing more painful for me than drinking was not drinking. I didn't think I was an alcoholic, I thought I was crazy. Telling him all this made him understand me all the more.

He told me that he had a wife and three boys (grown boys) that he loved dearly but they didn't want anything to do with him anymore as his drinking ruined that. He let me call my sister and she told me that she had been trying to get a hold of me. I went to her house and we all went down to the apartment where I had lived with Tracy and got my belongings. I told her what had happened, of course, she didn't think to highly of me. She told me that my ex-husband Joe had called and told me to be in court at the end of the month about Tracy, which was two weeks away. I tried my best to get my life in order but it just wasn't working. This friend agreed to go to court with me and pose as my boyfriend and help me get my daughter back.

Well, court day came and there I was drunk as a monkey and so was he. My sister was there also. All I can remember was that I stood up and cussed my ex-husband and the judge told me to sit down and be quiet. The decision was made that Joe and his wife would take Tracy to raise as I was considered an unfit mother to raise her. Tracy came to me and said "mom you are sick and when you get well I will come to see you". Joe said that I could call her before 11:00 PM anytime. That I could not see her until I got sober, as the court said if I stayed sober for 6 months I could get her back. I left the court totally in shock. I felt sick, hurt, hostile, remorse, you name it I felt so low down that I wanted to die. I started crying and my friend told me that he would help me get her back. We went home and got drunk.

By now this friend of mine, John, was running low in money and needed help with the rent in order to keep the apartment. He moved this guy in that had just come from detox. He had a job and helped the rent. He introduced to us a cheaper drink. It consisted of canned heat. Every day we went out and bought up all the canned heat we could find in drug stores, grocery stores, etc. We would also buy good linen handkerchiefs to strain the canned heat through. It was important to just strain the alcohol thru the handkerchief as the wax was considered very harmful. I was told you could go blind from it. This alcohol content was about 200 proof. We would mix it with orange juice or ice tea. Everyday we would make three pitchers of it. After straining it I would sterilize the handkerchiefs to reuse the following day. What a life. I stayed with John for a while and we were getting along pretty well. I was getting sick of nursing his problems and sat out front in the evening trying to meet some new people. I met a younger man who asked me to go to the beach with him. Now this was a challenge as I knew that I was free to do as I pleased. I had no real responsibilities. So without going back into the house, I left with this guy. We went to Richmond to some beach. We slept in the back of his truck, actually passed out. Come to find out his Grandmother lived there near the beach. We went over to meet her the next day, and she asked me to help get him into detox, as he had a physical problem. When he drank too much, he couldn't use his legs, which I found out in the morning.

I had to drive his truck over to his Grandmother's for him. She asked if I would leave him and go back where I came from. I agreed and she put me on a bus and gave me some money to catch a cab home when I got back in Arlington. When I got home John asked where I was and I told him a lie and he believed me and let me stay there again.

He said that his money had run out and we were going to have to find a place to stay. We went back to the rooming house in Alexandria and the lady there let us have a room for a short time only. I was really getting tired of his problems and wanted out. That night this man came to visit him from Florida and asked him to go shopping in Arlington with him. John told him that he was sick and needed a drink, so the guy got a bottle and off we went to go shopping. We went into one store and he told me to pick out anything I wanted. I bought some nice clothes. We left that store and went to this men's clothing store. John stayed in the car, as he said he was still sick. So I went with the guy into the store, thinking I could get some jeans there for myself. We picked out the clothes we wanted and went to pay for them. The guy pulled out a credit card to pay for the clothes, in the meantime this guy said you wait for the clothes and I'm going out to the car and get a drink. I waited and the salesman told me that they were getting the right size jacket so I waited. The next thing I knew the police were there to lock me up. I told them that something was wrong and they told me that the credit card was a stolen card.

They asked me where was the guy and I took them to the car to show them, but both of the guys were gone. They took me to jail and locked me up. They told me that the car was also stolen. They kept me in jail over night and released me the next day. They knew that I wasn't guilty.

They told me that I would be summoned to court later, as a witness. I went back to the rooming house and there was John. He told me that he didn't know that the guy had stolen the credit card and the car. Luckily I was free. Now the plan was to move again. This friend of Johns named Louis said he felt sorry for us the way the guy from Florida had done us so he offered to let us stay in his apartment building. This apartment ended up being in the Arlandria section of Alexandria. We went with him as we had no choice. We were there about a week and John said that he was going to have to leave town as the police were after him for that incident that happened. He left and went to Florida. This guy Louis told me I could stay with him.

So there I was again, with a total stranger. Funny after talking to him he turned out to be from my hometown, he seemed nice and he had a good job and kept me in food and booze. He took me to meet his mother who said she was very happy that he met a nice girl as he had been in so much trouble, especially drinking. By the way he wasn't drinking at the time. He also had been detox.

One day he asked me to go with him to buy a car and put it in my name as he had lost his license and couldn't drive. We went to buy the car at a dealership used car lot. I knew the guy pretty well that ran the place. We bought the car for $600 cash. About a week later the transmission started leaking very bad. We took it back and my buddy at the dealership agreed to fix it at no charge. I told him that I wanted a loaner until it was fixed and he let us have a brand new car. I drove it home and parked it. By the way Louis had started back drink now, and he was violent when he got drunk. It got so that he stayed drunk all the time and told me that I could not go anywhere without him and told everyone in the apartment building that I was to have no visitors. He beat me around a lot so I did just what he said.

Getting back to the car. When I got home I was tired and laid down to rest. He told the weird people that lived in the building to watch me and he would be back. It was just like I was in prison. At first I thought he was protecting me but found out differently. He took the car out for a spin while I was sleeping and wrecked it. He came back and woke me up and told me, I didn't believe him at first but when I saw it I was hysterical. He slapped me around and said that we were going to take the car back and park it next to the dealership and with the spare key we had he would pick up our car. Well, we did just that.

I was afraid of what would happen about the car and also afraid for my life with this character, but I had no choice. That night we sat out front and drank. Louis got into a fight with the weird people in the building and they actually started tearing a car apart in front of the apartment. They were throwing parts of the car at each other. They even took the railing to a fence in front of the building and ran up the stairs chasing one another with this log, breaking down doors and damaging the building bad. I ran into the bathroom and hid until it was over. By now I was so weak and afraid for my life, but I couldn't get away. I tried to run one time and he caught me and beat me badly.

Clearly a girl out in the streets (which was my situation) was separated from normal life in a variety of ways that even a male alcoholic could not understand. I was at the very bottom of the totem pole of respectability. What I did to exist robbed me of myself. Most people who have been around the alcohol/drug scene very long were convinced that rehabilitation of the female alcoholic was impossible because of what she had to do out in the world of alcohol and drugs. Life was a living hell now. Surely, I had hit rock bottom by now!

Louis bought some man to live at the apartment. He seemed very sick. I found out later that he had served time in prison. Louis and I took him to meet this couple. They talked over some kind of a plan to make big money, but of course, I didn't know this at the time. They would have me drive them to a small store in the surrounding metropolitan area and cash checks. They forced me to cash them as I had a driver's license to cash a check. This old man would sign these stolen checks that this couple had stolen from a construction company and make them out to me. Then they would send me into a store while standing at the door watching me with a gun hidden.

I was so afraid that they were going to shoot me. I told them one time that I was not going to cash any more checks and they beat me. They took me to a motel room and the man that had the gun took me by my feet and held me up in the air and beat me until I was black and blue. I ran away and hid out in a U-Haul truck until I couldn't stand it anymore as I was hungry, hurting and needed a drink bad.

I bummed a ride back to the apartment and when I got there, I looked like I was dead. Louis was in a good mood, I thought that he would beat me up again but he said that he would never have anything to do with that guy again. I believed him and he gave me a drink. He wouldn't let me eat anything though. I didn't eat much anyway, as all I lived on was wine. Now I was just a prisoner. I should have gone for help but was too sick from booze that I didn't know where I was half the time.

We were sitting out on the front porch one night, and a girl that lived in the apartment next door came over. She somehow got close enough to ask me why I was staying with those crazy people. I told her that I had tried to get away before but they would catch me and beat me. She told me that if I ever wanted to get away, that she would help me. I told her I would ask for help when I saw it was the right time.

That night Louis said let's go visiting one of his friends. It was a woman that lived close to the apartment. She was totally wiped out when we got there for a while and drank the guy from across the hall came over to drink too. He was a real nice man. He kept watching me and Louis picked up on that, so we had to leave. Before we left, this woman asked me if I wanted to come and live with her and I told her yes, if I could get away from Louis. She just said that I was welcomed without Louis hearing. We left and went back to the apartment.

Again we sat out front and that girl next door came over and asked me if I was ready to leave. I told her yes. She went into her house and got her husbands shotgun and held it at Louis and told me to run and don't look back. I did, and headed straight for that woman's apartment. When I got there, she wasn't there. I was frantic so I knocked on the man's apartment door that I had met. He let me in and I was crying. I told him what happened and he told me that I could stay there and no one would hurt me. I thanked him and he got me a drink and I stayed there for a week. His name is Toni. Toni told me that he had been jilted by a woman and that I could only stay there for a short time, as he didn't trust women.

I left the following week and went to a bar to meet some old friends that I knew. I told them that I needed a place to stay and this old man that lived next door took me in to take care of him and clean his house. I stayed there for a while until the old man started making passes at me. I told him no, and he pulled a gun on me and told me to get out and that I could not stay there unless I had sex with him. I grabbed what I that belonged to me as he had the gun pointed at me ready to shoot. I ran back to Toni's house and asked him if I could stay there until I got a job and he said that would be fine.

Well, now I have finally calmed down as Toni's place was peaceful and clean. He was a real nice person. I started to fall for him real bad, but I remembered that he said that he didn't want to get attached to a woman again.

CHAPTER 8

New Life

Toni and I started trusting each other, and he told me I could stay longer. I wasn't sure that I wanted to be with him. So one day while he was at work, I went out with the girl across the hall to visit some friends and party. Well, she left me there and I had no way home. I called Toni and told him what happened and he didn't believe me. He said she told him something different, yet I begged him to come get me. He finally did, and told me later that I would have to leave and he didn't want me at his place anymore. He figured that I had gone to be with this guy, but I didn't. I convinced him that I didn't and proved to him by getting this woman across the hall to tell him the truth and also tell him why she lied in the first place.

I did not have much to do with her from then on. Toni and I were getting along really good and one hot summer night, we had just finished dinner and were getting ready to set down and play some cards and drink, when there was a knock at the door. Thinking it was one of his friends, until I heard my name, and I thought it was Louis but it wasn't. It was the police and 4 detectives. They told me that I was under arrest and I had to come with them. I asked what for, and they told me petty larceny. I told them they had the wrong person and they showed me a copy of the check that had my signature and my social security number on it. I said yes, that's my signature, but I cashed that check for these people because they didn't have a driver's license to cash it themselves. I told them that I would never knowing walk up to a bank teller and cash a check that was bad. They told me to remain silent and come with them. Toni told me to go on and he would get me out. I changed into some decent clothes took a big water glass of whiskey before I left and a tranquilizer. The police asked Toni why I took so much and he told them that I was an alcoholic and would have a seizure if I didn't have the booze. They told me to tell the medic at the jail that, and that he would give me something to take to help me through it. By the time I got to Fairfax jail I was high. The police at the jail said is there anyone that you want to call before we lock you up as the bond was set so high that Toni couldn't afford to get me out yet. I called my sister, who lived by the jail. She told the police that she hoped that I rotted in jail and hung up. I cried.

Now, all I had in the world was Toni and he couldn't help me. They had to lock me up in the Arlington jail as they had no jail in Fairfax for women. I felt so sick and humiliated. They treated me like dirt there. I told them while I was going thru the procedures of being booked, that I was an alcoholic and please before they put me behind bars to give me something so I would not have a seizure. The doctor came and gave me some Librium. They put me in a big room where there was about 10 other women. I was afraid. They gave me a pillow and a mattress also a blanket to keep warm. I laid down and fell asleep. The Librium helped me. It felt like I was there only one day, but it had been three days. They woke me up to eat and give me more Librium during those three days. I had lost all thoughts of time. Those other women would come over and try to talk to me and I told them that I was afraid and was afraid that I was going to die in there. They laughed and made fund of me, but thank God, they left me alone.

I remember waking up a few times and seeing them doing funny things to each other and just turned over and ignored it. There was one girl who tried to commit suicide and they took her away. Finally, one the third day, they told me to get dressed, as I was going to court. When I got before the judge, he asked if I had any money to appoint an attorney, and I told him that a friend was trying to get me one, and he said take her back to jail until she gets a lawyer. I was sitting there with the bailer and I mentioned that my friend went to school with a lawyer in Fairfax, but I couldn't remember the name. Finally, the bailer mentioned a name, and I said that was it.

He immediately went to tell the court clerk and when he returned, he said the judge wants to see you in his chambers.

When I got to the judge, he asked me why I didn't mention the lawyers name in the court room, and I told him I didn't remember his name. They took me down to the holding room, and soon a real nice man walked in and said that he didn't know me, but he knew Toni very well, and any friend of Toni's could be trusted. He said he was a busy man and had to leave, but he would have a bondsman come down shortly and release me. I shook hands with him and thanked him and he left. Sure enough the bondsman came right after he left and released me.

The bondsman loaned me enough money to get home on the bus. Toni was surprised to see me, but also happy. I told him what happened and that I mentioned his friend, the lawyer. I had to go and see my lawyer, who worked for Toni's lawyer friend, and he took my testimony on tape. When he showed me some of the things all of these men I had met in the last 6 months had done, or were in to, I was shocked. They not only got me involved, there were other women with similar problems, that they used also in the this area as well as down south. When I was able to give them names and places, etc, they told me that the bank would probably let me go for the amount of the check that I cashed.

The check was for $295.00, and how sneaky it was that I was cashing a check for this young girl who was the girlfriend of one of those guys. I was told that she was loaning money to them so that they could pay their rent. It was her father's business check, it was blank and he had signed it. All they did was put my name in the payee and the I cashed it for them at the bank window with my driver's license. Little did I know that this girl was only 16, plus she had stolen the check from her father and forged his name, and the final blow was that I cashed it all not knowing this.

When the day came for court, I was told that I might possibly be facing one year in the state penitentiary. When the judge called my name, I was so scared, but he listened to what my lawyer had to say, and in turn, the judge looked at me and said "I am sentencing you to one year in the state penitentiary...SUSPENDED......providing that you do 3 things and in this order. You get a probation officer, get detox and go to rehabilitation and keep a clean slate for 1 year". He also said that looking at a woman 39 years of age, with 10 years working for the federal government, seemed to look as though I had a problem with alcohol. He then said case dismissed, but remember don't let me see you back in here within a year or you will go to jail.

I said thank you, and cried on my way out the door. I shook hands with my lawyer and caught the bus home. Oh what a relief. I was shaking so bad and really needed a drink. I couldn't wait until I got home to celebrate. Toni was so surprised and so happy to for me. I called the courthouse the next day, and got me a probation officer. It just happened to be a woman. She was real nice. She got me into the detox at Arlington Hospital. My stay there was to be 21 days. I thank God that it happened this way, as I don't think I would have gone for my on my own, but that I will never know. I do know that I really didn't want to stop drinking now, but I certainly didn't want to go to jail.

The biggest reason was because all of my friends drank and now I was all alone in the world. I had been to detox on my own back when Tracy had been taken from me, but I really didn't want to quit. I stayed in the hospital for the 14 days that time, and went back out and got drunk again. This time, the counselors ridiculed me about being back again, only to avoid going to jail. I wanted to leave by couldn't, as I didn't want to go to jail. I was a very stubborn hard-shell person now, I guess mainly from being around all of those street people that lived that as all their life. One part of me wanted to be my old respectful self but the other side just won every time, as I was ashamed of what happened to me while I was drinking. I thought I was the only one who had problems when I drank. My first day in the hospital was mostly sleeping and getting off the booze. I was sick and weak, but this time I was getting help.

It was clean, warm and quiet. About the fifth day, I was taken off all the drugs but still got my vitamins. There was always plenty to eat. We got three meals a day, plus a kitchen there with sodas, milk, juice, cold cuts to make sandwiches, and sweets for snacks between meals. We were not allowed to be in our room during the day. We had to go to classes, meetings, and sit in the game room or TV room. We could only go to our room at night to sleep. It was a whole new world you had to learn to live in. Reality is the hardest thing in the world to accept when you first come off alcohol. You cannot come to believe that you can ever do anything without alcohol. But this is where to begin, in detox, and I highly recommend it. It is the easiest way. Why fight it? Some studies show that there is one female alcoholic for every male. The female drinker is a quiet drinker usually, and that's why you don't hear too much about her. Most of the time the mid life woman abuses only herself. She does abuse her family in a passive sense; however, in that she often neglects their physical and emotional needs.

CHAPTER 9

Reality Check

Alcohol is a drug, a depressant of the central nervous system that is primarily detoxified in the liver. It produces either euphoria or a dulling of external, physical or psychic pain. Excessive and prolonged consumption can cause problems in the gastro-intestinal tract, including the liver, pancreas and esophagus. Female drinkers tend to have medical problems with less alcohol consumption than males. In other words, they get sick quicker. You are an alcoholic when your "social or occupational functioning" is impaired, when you are unable to control the amount you drink and the frequency with which drink it; when you develop a tolerance, which means it takes more booze to give you the same high' and when you have both mental and physical withdrawal symptoms including weakness, tremors, seizures, nightmares, confusion and insomnia. Most female alcoholics tend to become so in midlife, usually, in response to a loss. The loss maybe abstract, such as youth or sexuality; surgical, such as a breast or a uterus' or actual, such as a death, divorce or separation.

The loss is accompanied by depression, which is probably accompanied by a decrease in estrogen. The progression of alcoholism is rapid in females because there is a tendency to "telescope", or to process quickly from moderate to heavy drinking. The consequences, physical and mental, can be rapid also. Regarding attitudes and alcoholism, the alcoholic deteriorates into the general state of mind and feeling" certainly, altered, becoming increasingly negative. At first, these attitudes may not be observable, for example, she sneaks drinks with a sly concealing attitude as well as her drinking. In the eventual extreme behavior of the alcoholic, the attitude is apparent; no longer is it a minor secretiveness – now it is major, generalized network of lying, dishonesty, and cheating throughout all characteristics and attitude. When we experience self-doubt or guilt over our violations of acceptable way of behavior we reflect that negative feeling in our attitude towards others, ourselves and life itself.

This might not be understood by the inexperienced person in alcoholism or in therapy. What she sees as aggressiveness toward others may really be an attempt by the alcoholic to deny, to conceal his doubts and uncertainty. The general held attitude, feeling about alcoholism carries a stigma finds unacceptable to herself. Therefore, the alcoholic denies her alcoholism, so her reality becomes distorted and denied. She hurts, she is in pain, she says to herself, " I don't care; it can't be done; wait until tomorrow it's her fault; they don't understand me; why me?; I'm too sick; poor me". To reveal the "I do care, it can be done today, etc." To reveal this positive attitude would mean no more alcohol to deaden the hurt within, and people might reject her causing her more hurt. It's easier to stay with the other alcoholics outside of the mainstream. Her reality now is on a unconscious level. "If I blame them, I don't have to blame myself". She develops a negative attitude so as to avoid the painful struggle of coping with the alcoholism and with the stigma of being an alcoholic, creating more pain for herself and intensifying bother her inner and outward struggle to survive. Attitudes can be changing what she has been doing – old habits and former behaviors associated with drinking – gradually her attitudes are changed and thus she forms new values. Especially, the value of maintaining a life of sobriety, the value of serenity. We must recognize the need to change either ourselves, our behavior, our situation, or work, our social life and so on. Our behaviors in relation to others and our environment, or both. We must personally commit and be personally responsible to NOW – what we can do NOW as we cannot change the past. Our attitude should be one willingness to cope with reality.

Alcoholism causes Dis-Ease+ the definition of disease. Here are some more things that I learned about myself as an alcoholic while I was in the hospital.

Behavioral Patterns: intellect, rationalizing, justifying. It's not what alcohol does for us, it is what it does TO us. Whatever creates the problem, IS the problem. Emotional maturity, dependent, sensitive, idealist, impulsive, insecurity, tolorant and wishful thinking. All this makes the alcoholic stubborn and resentful. Recovery of alcoholism has got to be both the alcoholic and the non-alcoholic. Another problem is that the two of them will not talk realistic together. Children are enablers as they stay away form the alcoholic and the big problem is isolation. This is where you see children talking on the responsibility of the parent. The family is operating on a sick feeling they all have got to get well. Coming out of treatment – (Great Expectations) – the familyl has resentments toward the alcoholic because he or she is going to start taking over some of the responsibilities. Families must relate together and talk. At this point the non-alcoholic is the sicker one (emotionally). Communications is important now. Unless he or she gets honest with herself she cannot stay sober.

Sobriety means when we get it all together. Serenity is where we ourselves are altogether (oneness).

Three weapons an alcoholic has:

1) ability to arouse anger consciously it is his own self anger – the minute she knows it he turns you off.
2) ability to arouse anxiety on the part of the family. The family will do for the alcoholic what she must do for herself.
3) Love and compassion. The difference between a social drinker and an alcoholic is inability to stop and a physical compulsion. Alcoholism is physical, emotional and spiritual.

Early Warnings Are:

(1) increased tolerance
(2) Blackouts
(3) Abstinence for 2 or 3 days the alcohol is still there (you are still drunk)
(4) gulping drinks (others aren't drinking fast enough
(5) preoccupation – looking forward to the weekend, or party or stopping at a bar after work
(6) avoiding preference – getting upset at everything (at a point you usually get frequent blackouts)
(7) loss of control – irrepressible, not keeping promises, being pinned down to a specific time

(8) the first binge drink for 3 or 54 days and
quit for awhile (now has full control of the
bottle)

Massive State or Denial :

(1) Develops alibis.
(2) Reproof or remorse (If I can't drink, I'm not
a woman, etc.)
(3) Grandiosity behavior (working harder,
spending more, geographical change like
leaving the husband, job, etc.)
(4) Relatives enable her to drink then they
become afraid
(5) Finally threats of job, family, etc leaving.
(6) Ethical deterioration
(7) Alcoholi becomes bankrupt and everything goes. (Alcoholism has get her in full
strenghth)

Practicing Alcoholic

(1) Denial
(2) Counter-Denial
(3) Down Spiral
(4) Perfectionist
(5) Dependant upon alcohol

Enablers : rescues, makes excuses, cover-ups,
protects, adjusts and nurses.

Provokers: Husband or Spouse, the super nagger.

Victim: Boss, job, family and friends

Enough of the education of alcoholism for awhile. Getting back to my experience. After detoxification, I was informed to go to a rehabilitation house. I knew that I had to go there by order of the courts, but I wanted so bad to go out in the world and get my life going again, but they warned me that I needed to be around the winners....and not the losers.

I was pretty stubborn, even though I was sober. I felt that I was beyond my dignity to live in a halfway house. All my life, up to now, I was under the impression that a halfway house was where the bums stayed, and that I would have to sleep with one eye open. Well, as I said I had to go to the halfway house. Again, this was ordered by the courts. When I got there, I was afraid of everyone. I walked into the house and it had beautiful high ceilings and to my surprise, was very clean. There was a fireplace as well, and everyone welcomed me with open arms, and I felt right at home. I knew from here on that I needed this place as a start back to the life I once lived in my past.

They showed me to my room upstairs. The rooms all had 2 beds in them, and this was for a special purpose. They did not want you to be alone, which was similar to a hospital environment. I felt very nervous around the other clients. My fear was that they were better than me, as the state paid for my stay, and the other 14 women had some sort of a home or family to go back to.

My first 30 days were pure hell. I was assigned a chore to do every week. I would routinely get up at 6:00 AM, eat breakfast, then go about doing my chores. After my chores were finished, the rest of the day was mine. I sat around and read the big book, "Alcoholics Anonymous". I had no place to go but my room, so I read books and embroidered. I found a Serenity Prayer mat at a dime store, and spent most of my spare time embroidering.

Every night at 8:00 PM, I went to a meeting. This was mandatory. The meetings got boring and I wanted to so bad to stay home, but they would always say you went out drinking every night, so this is supposed to take that's place. Everyone kept picking at me because I wouldn't talk very much and never really tried to fix me up.

Finally, after 30 days, I was getting so tired of them nagging me, that I curled my hair one night, and came down to breakfast, and boy... what I reception I got. One of the other clients also talked me into praying every night. As what happened to me in the past, I felt that God wasn't there, as he never helped me when I asked him for something, he just never answered my prayers. The manager told me one day that I had better watch out for what I asked for, as I just might get it and then probably wouldn't be able to handle it.

My initial prayer was in the morning as I woke up, simply to Thank God for letting me live another day. As time went on in the house, I became more confident and found myself helping other new clients as they arrived. This is something I enjoyed very much. I got a lot of satisfaction helping others. Slowly, but surely, I could feel my confidence growing stronger. Soon enough, my manger figured that it was time for me to look for a job and start my program. I went looking for job after job and just ended up frustrated. I was getting impatient, and after about 3 months, I had outgrown the rehabilitation environment, I was approached by the Director to become the assistant manager. I would so happy, because now I would receive a paycheck. I told them I didn't think I was ready, and they said they wouldn't of picked me if I wasn't, so I accepted.

My job was to live in the other house that they managed, and in the mean time, I was able to see my boyfriend on the weekends. They were afraid that I would slip back into my old ways because my boyfriend was still drinking. I assured them that if he got to be too much for me, I would leave. I had to do that on two different occasions. As soon as I got my first paycheck, I went out and bought some new clothes. When I first came to the halfway house, all I had was the clothes on my back. Charity had donated some clothes to the house, and I found a few outfits that fit me until I was able to get a job and buy my own clothes. This was a very rewarding job and I really loved helping others.

Just like anything else in life, I soon out grew this type of environment and felt that it was time for me to live with my boyfriend. I put in my resignation and went to live with him, and although he was drinking, it didn't bother me because I no longer had the desire to drink. He respected my sobriety but still raised hell when he had too much to drink. I look back now and see that I could possibly of made a mistake of living with him, as I got upset when he would drink heavy and then would wish I were back in the halfway house.

Funny though I knew that I had to learn to cope with problems without drinking. I managed to do this, but was very nervous after my boyfriend had a drinking binge. I am inclined to believe that once you have lived in this sort of situation, you seem to return back to that same way of life, such as; living around my Dad that drank and my ex boyfriend who drank and now my new boyfriend who also drank. It seems that I have felt that I must be the head of the household…just like my mother…and to date, that has been my pattern. My boyfriend and I stayed at that apartment for one year together, and then moved to a better apartment that was unfurnished. We did this after I got a job back with the government. Again, I was feeling very confident about myself.

While I was at the halfway house I bought a used car for $25, what a steal. The only thing was that it smoked bad, but to me it was transportation. My boyfriend got his Aunt's old car as she bought a new one. So I sold my car. By the way, my boyfriend was separated from his wife for 12 years but legally never got a divorce. To date I have accepted it and in a way am glad that we didn't get married, as over the years his drinking has progressively gotten worse. His sister started selling real estate and convinced us that we should buy a home. Well, we found a nice house and figured that we would get married after we moved into the house.

Well, we are still living in the house but now we have separate bedrooms. His alcoholic ways has made us so far apart. He keeps saying that some day he is going to quit but it never happens. I keep having mixed emotions about leaving him as I remember back when I didn't have a family or a friend and he stuck by me and I felt obligated to stay and help. But, slowly I have different feel about staying. He never goes anywhere with me anymore. I don't get out much other than work. I keep feeling that there has got to be some peace of mind out there somewhere for me. This is where I have to go back and discipline myself. I must get away from him and go to some meetings. I need someone to talk to about how I feel.

AA Program is sharing hope, strength and experiences, and in solving my problems. The desire to stay sober so my way of staying alive because I know in my heart that if I take that first drink again that it will be all over for me again. Sobriety means self-possession in Latin. Guilt is a thermometer of my values. I have learned that group discussions with the others and challenging others as well as them challenging me about my past, my old ways when you think of drinking or giving up.

At first, I thought that by them forcing me to talk about my past was cruel, and until I broke down and cried they kept reminding me how important it was to get it all out in the open, that that was the only way to stay sober and survive. I had insomnia all night about all the bad things I did and was glad I had someone to talk to until the feelings passed. It was hard for me to accept the fact that I had to forget my good past as well as the bad for a while and give up the idea of getting my little girl back. They told me to accept the fact that I might never get her back. To accept the fact that I failed to and go on from there. I cried many nights over this. If I hadn't been on probation, I think I would have left the house and gone back out on the streets. But I kept telling myself that these people wouldn't keep telling me these things unless they cared.

This was hard for me to realize that someone cared for me. After all the bad things I did. I couldn't accept affection at first or be kind to people. When I finally did, it felt funny, but I got a natural high from it. I was constantly reminded to stop lying and cheating. Honesty was the only survival, no matter how it hurt. I was reminded to stay away from old friends and learn to make new friends that weren't from my past. They kept a check on me just like a cop, all the time, but this was good, and I needed that for awhile, to keep me straight.

Eventually, my attitude toward sobriety was becoming an obsession. To explain, this means that once you have developed your program, you tend to get selfish at first, and I remembered how worried I was when I felt this happening. I was told that I was getting it all together, after the long hard struggle for life, to be free of the nasty burden of drunkenness and guilt and all that goes with that. I actually felt like a large crater had been lifted off my back. The time had come when there was hope and I could see the light at the end of the tunnel.

Looking back, alcohol permitted me to do things I was very shy, alcohol made me feel 8 feet tall. I can see now that the only trouble in the home was alcohol, and very early one, I blamed people, places and things...which was convenient to do. I would quit drinking at different times for different reasons. When around people in any setting, I could always search people out in a crowd that drank. I was a periodic drinker at first. I would evidently start just weekend drinking and then later it started Thursday of every week. There were many embarrassing situations, many injuries and some arrests. Those didn't seem bad.

The worst was the internal injury, internal failures, guaranteed failures, always looking over your shoulder, constant failures. I knew there was something wrong but didn't know what it was. There was a constant compulsion of never ending to drink. The mystery of it all is that the most people that drink, only one in ten become an alcoholic. What distinguishes the difference between the rest is still a mystery. Investigators have diagnosed that early symptoms are subtle and allusive. Alcohol tends to be a friend at first, as it helps you accomplish things. It's a hard relationship to explain to people who haven't experienced it themselves.

Alcohol to most people in a social setting is one drink, but to an alcoholic, this sounds totally silly. One drink?? They just as well not go to that event if for only one drink. Alcohol distorts all that is normal in life. I always felt uncomfortable at family outings, I hated holidays and getting together, as I felt depressed at those settings, I didn't feel part of it. Now that I am well and on my way to recovery, I can see that the world that was abnormal at the time I was drinking, seemed normal at the time.

For instance, I remember a bartender friend told me once (after telling him that I must of put away a lot the night before) that I had three tumblers of triple martini's. The funny part of it was that I remember driving home. This is where the physiological addiction develops, periodic drinkers, binge drinkers, blackouts, etc. Gulping drinks or drinking reinforcement before going to a party. Loss of control develops. Some people cannot keep up with how much they drink, which is a very scary situation. Withdrawals develop, tremors, irritability, depression and other undesirable feelings.

Alcoholics are depressed because they drink and if they don't drink, they're depressed. Alcohol causes an altered psychological state of being. For instance, when arriving at an emergency room because of some seemingly signs of breakdown of the nervous system, the patient is diagnosed as being overworked or a mental disturbance. In the past, doctors always diagnosed the patient as so, it never entered their mind that the patient could have an alcohol problem, and so the doctor prescribed tranquilizers. Now the patient is cross addicted even if the doctor would have asked the patient how much he or she drank, and the patient would always lie, or he or she didn't want the doctor to know about their problem.

I would like to tell you a funny story about the liver, but the end result is scary. This is the way it was told to me, it was funny, but the end left me to believe that it was high time for me to really consider quitting the booze. Weighing in at 3 or 4 pounds, the liver is the largest of the glands. It's spreading crown of tissue continuously draws nourishment from the blood vessels of the intestine. Manufacturing a pint of bile a day, without which golden liquor we could not digest, so much as a single raisin. The human body is perfectly suited for the ingestion of alcohol and it's rapid utilization, in that sense, we are not unlike alcohol lamps. Endless is our eagerness to devour alcohol.

Witness the fact that it's absorbed, not only from the intestine, as are all other foods, but directly from the stomach. Once incorporated into the body, it is the liver that has the task of oxidizing the alcohol. Even the sturdiest of livers can handle only a drop or two at a time, and the remainder swirls endlessly in the bloodstream, and is exhaled by the lungs and thus provides the state police with a cracker jack method of detection in measuring the presence and amount of alcohol ingested. One martini increases the fat content of the liver sufficiently so that it can be seen by the use of special strains under a microscope. In other words, a single martini increases the fat in a liver by one half percent of the weight of that organ, above the normal 3%.

In the alcoholic, this commonly reaches a death defying twenty five percent. You don't have to be an alcoholic to get cirrhosis. Some quite modest drinkers get it. The state of nutrition is also a factor in the development of cirrhosis. It is no secret that boozers, the serious kind, stop eating, especially protein, either because they can't afford it or because the sick liver just can't handle the metabolism of protein well, and the appetite is warned off. The nitrogenous material of protein passes directly through the diseased liver and exerts a toxic effect on the brain. If one restricts protein in the diet of cirrhotic, the brain improves. The avoidance of exercise and sitting around guzzling up the suds soon becomes the wrecking ball of cirrhosis.

The roofs and walls and hallways, complaining under their burden of excess fat, groan and buckle. Inflammation sets in, and whole roomfuls of liver cells implode and die. And in their place comes the scarring that twists and distorts the channels, pulling them into impossible angulations. Avalanches block the flow of bile tangles of fiber impede the absorption and secretion. This happens not just in one spot but over, until the gigantic architecture is a mass of sores and wounds, the old ones scarring over as new ones break down. The obstructed bile, no longer able to flow down the gut, backs into the bloodstream to light up the skin and eyes with the sickly lamp of jaundice. The stoop turns to toothpaste while in commiseration, the urine dark as wine. The belly swells with gallons of fluid that weep from the surface of the liver. The entire body is discommoded. The blood fails to clot, the palms of the hands turn mysteriously red, the spidery blood vessels leap and crawl on the skin of the face and neck. Male, breasts enlarge, and even the proud testicles turn soft and atrophy. In a short while, the impotence develops, and irretrievable form of impotence which may well produce the invalid into more and more drinking.

Scared???? Better have a drink. You look a little pale. In any case, there is not need to be so glum. Especially if you know something I know. Liver tissue will regenerate, yours will and regain all it' old efficiency and know how. All it requires is quitting the booze now and then.

The ever grateful, forgiving liver will respond joyously with a multitude of mitoses and cell divisions. This rejuvenation is carried out with the speed of a starfish growing an new ray from the stump of the old. Soon the big house is humming with activity again, and all those terrible things I told you happen, go away...all except that impotence thing. Well, you didn't expect to get away scott free, did you? Here's something to tuck away and think about whenever you want to feel good....60% of all cirrhotic who stop drinking will be alive and well five years later. How unlink the lofybrain, which has no power of regeneration at all. Once a brain cell dies, you are forever one shy. Good old liver!

Many people think the only health problems related to alcoholism are painful hangovers, cirrhosis of the liver, or in extreme cases...delirium tremens. Not so. Prolonged alcohol abuse also affects the heart and other muscles, the brain, glands and digestive tract. One the other hand, moderate use of alcohol can be socially, psychologically, and even physically beneficial. Keep in mind that alcohol is an anesthetic addictive drug. The same substance that can rely on, can also put you in a deep sleep, and in sufficiently large doses, cause death. No one has been able to prove that responsible drinking is harmful to the health of most people. The key is moderation. Like nearly everything else, too much liquor is a dangerous thing. Calorie conscious Americans already know alcohol is fattening. Many may not be aware that heavy alcohol intake deprives the body of valuable protein, vitamins, and minerals. When hunger pains are satisfied by the empty calories of alcohol, less food is eaten, and nutrition suffers. In addition, heavy alcohol consumption interferes with food absorption, so even if the heavy drinker eats well, he may have borderline or actual malnutrition. A muscle disease called alcoholic myopathy is sometimes found in patients with a long history of alcohol abuse. The symptoms are severe muscle cramps, swelling, and in later states, fragmentations of muscle fibers. Chronic cases display muscle weakness. After drinking heavily over a period of time, signs of brain and nerve malfunction may occur, including acute and chronic hallucinations, disorientation as to time and place, and memory and reasoning failures. Some of these symptoms are directly related to the common vitamin deficiencies of the alcoholic person, and respond favorable to massive doses of vitamins, especially the B variety. Alcoholism can produce an enlarged, flabby heart muscle, a condition that often leads to congestive heart failure.

On a somewhat encouraging note, studies indicate that alcohol is not a significant risk factor in heart attacks. Interestingly, moderate drinkers as a statistical group have a lower rate of heart attacks than abstainers. Chronic heavy drinking has a harmful effect on the entire digestive system. Digestion problems, problems, ulcers, and inflammation of the pancreas are common complaints. Also, heavy drinking is strongly correlated with the development of cancer of the mouth and throat, especially if combined with heavy smoking. A heavy drinker who does not smoke has nearly the same increased risk of developing these cancers is a heavy smoker who does not drink.

Here is the formula as to when to say when in drinking. A drinking problem can be measured not only be how much one drinks, but also how and why. Using alcohol to relieve everyday pressures, to cope with fears, or to escape loneliness are some of the early signs of dependence on alcohol. Some others are: starting the day with a drink, going to work intoxicated, being criticized for our drinking by an employer, spouse, or others, making excuses for your drinking behavior "I need just one more to relax", undergoing dramatic personality and behavioral changes after drinking, driving a car while intoxicated, coming into a conflict with the law as a result of drinking or requiring medical attention or suffering frequent phsycial discomfort because of drinking. Those who abuse alcohol and get drunk are overdosing with a drug. Because of the magnitude of the misuse of alcohol in country, alcohol abuse and alcoholism is our number one drug problem today.

Communication of factual, unbiased information is the purpose of this story. I believe that the decision whether to drink alcohol or not is a personal decision that each American must make for themselves. If they decide to abstain, others should respect that decision. If you choose to drink, you should know how to use alcohol to enhance human relationships – not destroy them. We, as a nation, need to agree on what is responsible use of alcohol. For the most part, we do not know how to drink, our own hang-ups and ignorance about alcohol not only perpetuates bad examples and dangerous practices, but also make it more difficult to recognize a drinking problem in it's early stages when we see one. We are told frequently these days that we must have lost our ability to determine our own destinies.

It is clear that every American can shape a part of his future by adopting a responsible attitude toward the use of alcohol – and by promoting that attitude among those close to those who drink. We can help change the guilt-ridden attitude that proves our current use of alcohol. Change is necessary. Someday, hopefully, in the not too distant future, there will be good news about alcohol. You know it's funny. The way booze is built up you'd think that the first drink was the pot of gold at the end of the rainbow or some magic key to independence and never ending good times. After that first drink, some people like to think: "Alright, I've made it now. No more telling me what to do. If I can drink, I must really have it all together." Only trouble is, it doesn't quite work out that way.

Try walking to the end of the rainbow and you'll probably find some guy changing a flat tire. It's the same way with a drink. There's nothing wrong with it, but it doesn't hold any special secrets either. It's just a drink. Although alcohol is a drug that can be dangerous if misused, it's ingredients are nothing to get excited about. It's a chemical compound made from some pretty basic stuff : yeast, water and sugar. That makes it about as mysterious and exciting as mouthwash. What's important is what you use the alcohol for.

Now that's worth talking about. Some uses of alcohol are:

1) Training homing cockroaches
2) To power a scale model of the Second World War
3) To relax or to celebrate or to warm up a conversation

There's nothing wrong with that. A drink is fine as long as not too much importance is attached to it. As long as you don't need it to have a good time, or as long as the people you're with are more important that the drink in your hand. Trouble begins only when the drink itself is what a person is most interested in. Some people drink not to make a good time better, but to kill time or escape from problem. Then, drinking becomes a sickness. How do some people get hooked on drinking? A few drinks can make a person feel more confident, more adult, and less hassled by problems and pressures. But once that nice, smooth, on top of the world feeling wears off the drinker still has the same problems starting him in the face. In the end, heavy drinking is the best way to keep a person from finding out who she or he is. Of course, each person has to decide for himself what's good for him or her, but when someone is doing a lot of drinking, it's pretty easy to see that they are doing less and less of the things he used to get a kick out of.

Since drinking has nothing to do with being cool or sophisticated or adult, it does many sense to look down on people who don't drink. Everybody has the right to decide for themselves whether to use alcohol or not, so when the time comes to make a decision about drinking, give your friends a chance to be themselves. While you're at it, do it for yourself to.

This has been my only way of coping with the real world. Whatever seems to have become a burden in your life, release it now. Put it in God's hands. Put every person, every challenge, every decision, your dear ones, your home, your health, your business, your goals, and your past, present and future in his hands. Let me assure you right now that God's wisdom is abundantly able to handle all things wonderfully well. God's love is infinite and all consuming, and his peace is ever present and read to comfort, uplift and heal. Listen within, and let the light of Spirit guide you and direct you. You will find great peace stealing through your being.

This manner of prayer was my rod and my staff day by day, during a time when I needed to make not only one, but several very vital decisions in my life. I knew that I needed to put every detail into God's hands. I found the inner peach and desire and was guided above and beyond my highest expectations. Every outcome unfolded in order, harmony, and with enrichment for me. The hands of God work through our hands. To put anything in God's hands is to take it above the confusion of the human limitations and to place it in a new environment of mind and heart where the reality of God is released and miracles occur.

In order to help yourself, deliberately, insistently, continually turn from any appearance that seems to hinder your progress or deny your good. Stay attended to the idea of putting all details into the hands of God and leaving them there. As you practice this attitude and develop this habit, you will begin to establish a stronger awareness of the closeness of God's help and the reality of His presence within you.

MY OPINION OF ALCHOHOLIC ANONYMOUS (AA)

From time to time, I was asked if I wanted to help and what a tragic end to my alcoholic ego! I wanted to help, alright, but my pride (false pride) interfered with asking for help or accepting it.

My opinion of AA has been poor to start with, but it fell on a new low after seeing these drunks recommending to me to go for help at AA, that once helped them and they were drunk again. This was very confusing. Full of self pity and will, a completely negative outlook on life, I bemoaned my terrible fate. As much as I denied the help of the group, they had certain traits to their credit. They showed a genuine interest in my predicament and spoke my language without preaching to me. Assurance brought little hope to me. I was so exhausted, both physically and mentally, I could neither agree or disagree nor fight back, so I went along with the program and went to the hospital, wondering what would happen next.

It came time for me to leave and it was suggested to go to a halfway house. With my stinking thinking, I said I didn't need that and I could handle myself okay, but when I got out into the world all alone, with no one, I panicked and got a bottle and got drunk. Then I ended up in trouble. This time returning to the hospital and determined to accept the program fully the second time around. A guilty conscious complicated my morbid fears. My spirit seemed broken beyond repair, but with such mentality as I had left, I decided it would be more profitable to join AA than to prolong hellish suffering along.

It was easier to be able to go to the medical facility than going cold turkey as well as the fact that alcoholism is treated as an illness rather than a sin. One thing that is hard to understand is that when you ask for help and there is no room available at the hospital, you are instructed to drink at least 2 ounces of whiskey every hour until a room is available. Although medical treatment was required, the crux of my incredible success depended upon the spiritual condition. Will power was not a factor of my recover, as my only will was to drink. It should be called won't power. I decide that help had to come from some power greater than alcohol, and I chose God. It was an honest and sincere choice, but it presented many obstacles as it called for total surrender of certain character defects. This was very hard to do.

Many times, I learned at AA that people were insane to do this. I thought to myself I certainly kept my sanity. Surprisingly enough, I realized later that all the crazy things I did, that I could remember, were crazy or definitely insane.

When it came time to accept the third step, turning my life over to God, I wasn't too sure I wanted to do that as when I was drinking, I asked him to help and it seemed he didn't care. The early stage of my sobriety, I was a little hesitant about accepting God, but now I pray for his help every day. The fourth step I really enjoyed. I made an inventory of good and bad character- istics that served to over come my obstinacy and to lessen my battle against surrender.

The fifth step is admitting to God and one other person of my wrong doings. This I was sure that I would never admit to another person, because of my bad record, and I didn't want to be humili- ated. I found out that when I did tell another person, I felt so much better with the knowledge of being forgiven. Now that I am sober, I figured that because I was not drinking anymore, I was cured of alcoholism. After being sober in AA, you'll hear of those who slipped, but you are always welcomed back. You can even get to thinking that you proved that you can take it or leave it alone, but this is just that old stinking thinking or drinking thinking again.

Regarding the eighth step, most of us refrain from making a list of those we hurt or harmed because of fear. I made my list and it wasn't too hard to do once I became submissive enough to realize the need for compliance with this step. When I took the ninth step, my experience was going to my sister's house, I had abused, hurt and taken advantage of her for so many years. I was afraid that they would ridicule me or even kick me out. I got the confidence and help for this visit by discussing it in AA. I had to lead a meeting one night, so I discussed this problem. I got plenty of help that night.

When I visited my sister, it was nice, but I didn't stay long the first time. I wanted to see them, and then continue to keep in touch, to assure them I wasn't drinking anymore. My next step was to see my daughter who was staying with my ex husband out of state. I wrote her a letter and got the most wonderful letter back. I still have it today. She was happy that I was okay, and most of all....still alive. The last time she saw me, I was in bad shape. A year later, her Dad allowed her to come and visit me for two weeks. It was a step toward mending those wrongs I did to her. At first, my daughter preferred to stay with her Dad, but her visits got longer and longer. I could have taken the case back to court, and gotten custody, but I didn't want to be selfish and I was happy enough with the situation. I now have my daughter living with me permanently. Patience is a virtue.

On the tenth step, I continued to take inventory of myself and other people and there was a rewarding feeling of partial accomplishment and a sense of well being. Some members follow step ten's suggestions and thus retain their sobriety. At first, I carried the middle of the road attitude which made me question the advisability of total adherence to any of the AA steps. This half-hearted effort divorced me from alcohol, but made me irritable and unhappy. My attitude did not directly oppose the practice of the eleventh step, but did lack sufficient stimulus for deep reflection on God's will.

My opposition over step eleven was overcome by thoughts of my helplessness and desperation before going to AA. I discussed this with my group, and kept praying every day. My first attempts were feeble and weak, but they got me started upon a daily spiritual procedure, which made the difference between success and failure. It was a stimulating experience. My whole concept on life stated to change for the better. I got a zest for living, which I never had before. I was filled with a desire for my future sobriety and help other alcoholics. I learned good things happening were not always permanent.

Step twelve predicts real spiritual attainment for members who live the AA program. It suggests that we work with other alcoholics and continue a spiritual way of life in all of our daily activities.

Being spiritually awakened opens a door for us to be happier and lead a sober life. Though we have faith that God will use us as instruments to carry out his will, our job is to be willing and ready to accept the opportunities as they present themselves to us. He does not promise to remove all our problems, but when we put our trust in Him, He does make possible a harmonious way to either overcome them, or to avoid them. We are not forced to live by step twelve by god. He simply grants us sobriety if we are consistent in our daily practice.

Fear, dishonesty, resentment and reservations are a few of the mental blocks which impede our progress in the AA way of life. These emotions often cause us to drink again. People tend to inflict us with mental drunkenness which comes from a form of fear, anger, dishonesty, resentment, jealousy, hatred and mental or physical exhaustion. We find enough excuses we consider legitimate, to stop reading the Big Book, and to keep us from meetings, then we are in real trouble.

Alcoholics form bad habits easily, and quickly form the habit of not reading the Big Book, or coming to meetings at all. A member who is mentally drunk has the bad habit of getting physically drunk and dropping out of AA. Without spiritual help, self will takes over and becomes a short cut to renewed drunkenness. The twelve steps have taught us a way of life which we can combat our harmful emotions and devote the strength of our minds to attaining happy contented sobriety. Successful members soon learn to recognize barriers as they study the Big Book and try to live by the Twelve Steps. We will have problems, many problems, but with God's help, and the practice of AA, we will sublimate these problems, which might enslave us to alcoholism.

We are still and will always be alcoholics.